We Who Worship

by

Cheryl Salem

Unless otherwise indicated, all scripture quotations are taken from the *New Spirit-Filled Life Bible*. Copyright © 2002, by Thomas Nelson. Used by permission. Scripture within text appears in italics.

We Who Worship
ISBN 1-890370-22-3

Published by Salem Family Ministries
PO Box 701287
Tulsa, OK 74170

Introduction 5

The Heart of a Worshiper.............................. 9

Worship in Spirit 19

Worship in Truth 29

Guard the Heart of Worship 43

A Prepared Worshiper................................ 57

A Praying Worshiper 69

A Humble Worshiper 85

A Pure Worshiper 101

A Worshiper of Integrity 109

An Accountable Worshiper 119

A Submissive Worshiper 127

An Authoritative/Disciplined Worshiper 135

Being Worship 149

Restoration of Worship 155

Heaven and Earth Worship 163

Wordless Worship and Weeping Worship 169

Prophetic Vision of Worship 181

We Who Worship

Purpose:

To raise up worshipers *with a* clean heart, *called to be* instruments of worship *by the Holy Spirit.*

Introduction

Purpose: To raise up worshipers with a clean heart, called to be instruments of worship by the Holy Spirit. To define the innate difference between worshiper and musician, singer, dancer, artist, performer, etc. This school of worship is for those who are willing to lay down their lives, to be completely His, to live and to be used by Him with humility, purity, integrity, and accountability.

This statement of purpose has been written for a long time in my journals, notes, and computer files. It is for a school, a school of worship. It is not merely a school to train musicians how to better perfect their gifts and talents, but a school to better equip a person to stand long-term, in the high, called position of worshiper. Worship is not just confined to the platform or the pulpit. Worship is not assigned only to those with a microphone or an instrument. Worship is relationship.

It is not just about music, or talent, or gift. This school is about the heart. The heart of a worshiper is what draws the attention of God from the heavenly throne to earth's footstool.

Isaiah 66:1
Heaven is My throne,
And earth is My footstool.

It is the heart of a person that beckons the Worshiped to come to the worshiper. It is the heart of a worshiper that responds to the One who is worshiped in answer to His call of "*Come!*"

Revelation 22:17
And the Spirit and the bride say, "Come!" And let him who hears say, "Come!"

What is in the heart of man? Only God knows for sure.

Psalm 44:21
Would not God search this out? For He knows the secrets of the heart.

It is not my intention to try and know the heart of others, rather to challenge the minds of others to check and re-check their own hearts. The further we go from the truth of a pure heart the longer it will take us as a society to find our way back. Why am I writing this book? It is the first step to obeying God and His command upon my life to raise up worshipers who will worship Him with a pure heart. I believe this school of worship will help equip the called to fulfill their destinies at His feet.

This is a school of heart first, then of thought and purpose. It begins with these pages. From here, I am not sure where He will lead, but I am certain He will lead, and that's enough for me. He gives the orders, I obey.

The longer I serve the Lord, the more I know that I am on a 'need to know' basis, and most of the time, to follow His instructions and obey His voice, I don't need to know! My purpose is not to know everything. My purpose is to obey the One who knows everything, everywhere!

As you read, I suggest you continually pray and ask the Lord to show you what He longs for you to know. Ask the Father to reveal to you His specific purpose, for you, in this great scheme of life. Where do you fit as a worshiper? What are you doing right? What do you need to change to come closer to His throne and bow down before Him?

He will show you. It may take a lifetime. But it is not solely about the destination as much as it is about the journey. Worship is not about the bottom line, or the attaining of a position or a place. Worship is about the romance of God and His people. *(I am my beloved's, and my beloved is mine. Song of Solomon 6:3)*

Come with me and we will worship the King together. Look for me! I will meet you at His feet!

Come with me
and we will
worship the King
together.
Look for me!
I will meet you
at His feet!

Chapter One
The Heart of a Worshiper

John 4:23-24
But the hour is coming, and now is, when the true worshipers will worship the Father in spirit and truth; for the Father is seeking such to worship Him. God is spirit, and those who worship Him must worship in spirit and truth.

> *Worship is about pureness of heart.*

We who worship must understand the true meaning of the word, "worship." When we do not truly know what worship is, then how can we do it? And quite possibly even more important than actually 'doing' worship, the real question is this; when we do not truly know what worship is, then how can we *be* it?

Worship is not an action as much as it is a heart response. God is looking for those who are responding heart to heart with Him. He is looking and searching the entire earth's surface for those who will respond to Him in adoration and exploration of intimacy, without restraints or any thoughts of self-preservation. Worship can never be about the worshiper, rather totally and completely about the Worshiped.

Worship is not about giftings or talents. Worship is not about the best instrument or the best voice. Worship is not about the most trained of musicians, dancers, artists or performers. Worship is about pureness of heart. The motives with which we approach the throne of God have everything to do with the pureness of our worship.

I am reminded of a time in the early 1990's when I was having angelic visitations and encounters on a regular basis. On one such occasion, we were in a service and the angels filled the sanctuary. There is nothing more hair-raising or spine-tingling than a room being charged with the actual presence in the atmosphere, of supernatural, heavenly beings!

The angels stood shoulder to shoulder as if at attention, flanking around the top of the room. I use the verb 'stood' as a broad and relative term, since in our natural realm they were actually suspended in mid-air, standing on nothing seen with the natural eye. After a few moments, an angel stood behind me, tapping me on the shoulder to get my attention. As I turned around, I fully expected to be gazing into the face of a human being, having no idea that words were about to be spoken from the eternal realm that would change my thinking and my being for the rest of my life! This gigantic, light-filled angel said to me, "Write this down! You have often wondered why we appear at different times in the service. We are released to come in when the praise becomes pure. Not when you think it is pure, but when God knows it is pure by the hearts of the people. Then we are allowed to come in and do our jobs."

My life, my thinking, and my perception of worship was forever changed from that moment forward. So, what happens in any given service, meeting, or gathering of believers is not about God withholding from us His Spirit, His angels, His anointing, His healing, etc. What happens in any given service is dependent upon the pureness of our hearts as we worship the King of kings and the Lord of lords. When our hearts are pure towards Him, and He knows it (and He always knows our hearts, even when we don't know our own motives! He always knows our conscious and our subconscious thoughts!), He releases whatever it is we need to go to the next level, the next position in the eternal realm of living and being. It is about the pureness of who we are. The pureness of our worship tells the level of the pureness of our sacrifice to Him on the altars of our lives.

Worship has many different actual and perceived definitions. Let's take a look at one of them. In the *New Spirit-Filled Life Bible,* there are particular passages that are expounded upon using certain Hebrew and Greek definitions. Many of these are called Word Wealth sections throughout this particular type of Bible. In Revelation 4:10, there is a Word Wealth section that gives the following explanation concerning the word, "worship."

"Worship," "proskuneo" pronounced (pros-koo-*neh*-oh). *Strong's Concordance* #4352 (Greek in origin). From pros, "toward," and kuneo, "to kiss." "To prostrate oneself, bow down, do obeisance, show reverence, do homage, worship, adore." In the New Testament, the word especially denotes "homage rendered to God and the ascended Christ." All believers have a one-dimensional worship, to the only Lord and Savior. We do not worship angels, saints, shrines, relics, or religious personages.

So one meaning of worship would be to *kiss toward.* In our society it could mean to *blow kisses! (I am my beloved's, and my beloved is mine! Song of Solomon 6:3)* God is looking for, He is searching the entire earth over, for one who will love and worship Him! When I see Him, I light up; my eyes widen with delight, and I can't wait - even the time it takes for me to cross the room to embrace Him is too long! I quickly purse my lips in the shape of a kiss even as my hand is coming to my lips!! Without hesitation of embarrassment or shame in any sense of the word, I blow a kiss across the distance and space of the room toward my Beloved! I worship Him, close or far; I worship Him when I am less than a breath away or when it feels thousands of miles apart. I worship Him!! I close the perceived distance between us by blowing Him kisses!

In our society of so-called worship services, there are paid and unpaid worshipers. We call them many things: musicians, singers, dancers, worship leaders, worship pastors… the list goes on and on. But with all the titles, microphones, and amplification, do we have any true worshipers in the house of God? As a performer for many early years, and now a true worshiper without performance for humanity to applaud, let me ask you, which one are you?

When a worshiper, whether self-proclaimed or otherwise, leaves the platform after the worship portion of the service is finished, the questions should not be:

"Did I lead the people in worship?"
"Did I do well?"
"Did I sing beautifully?"
"Did I play my instrument accurately?"
"Did I dance or do my drama with blah, blah, blah?"

The questions should be:

"Did I worship God in spirit and in truth?"
"Did I touch the throne of God?"
"Did I touch the hem of His garment?"
"Did I abandon my desire to please humanity and only please my Creator?"
"Did He hear the sound of my worship so high in the spirit that only my Bridegroom could know the sound of His bride?"
"Did I sing as if no one was listening?"
"Did I dance as if no one was watching?"
"Did I use every fiber of my being: spirit, soul, and body, to worship the King of kings without the constraints of worrying what any human might think or say?"

The term, "worship leader," is missing the point completely! People can no more be "led to worship" than they can be led anywhere else! As a parent, one of the great truths I learned is that children do not do what you tell them to do, they do what you do! They watch you, they see you, and they imitate you. That's how they learn. I am not saying that our worship does not cause others to want to enter in to worship with us. I am not saying that it is not a great opportunity to help another person find their way to the throne of God. I am saying that worshiping the Lord is much like going to sleep. No matter how many people try to help me, when it comes right down to it, I either enter into sleep or I don't. I used to tell our son, Roman, at bedtime, "Son, going to sleep is a one man job." There is truly no one else who can help me worship, nor is there anyone who can stop me! Worship is a choice of my will.

When it comes to worshiping the Lord, we must understand that many people are too "into themselves" too prideful, too embarrassed, too self-absorbed to be led anywhere, especially led to the feet of Jesus, to bow down, to get low enough to not be seen or heard. Pride will cause many people to actually dig in their heels when there is the slightest pull on their being to "get over themselves." One must willingly come to worship the King. We do have the great opportunity and privilege as worshipers, to allow those who long to come to His feet to join us as we worship. But no matter how much I long to help everyone find their way, find their place at His feet, it is still ultimately the sole responsibility of the seeker to find the One whom they seek! We can show by example, when our hearts are pure, the amazing power of His presence. We can invite any and all to join us. But we cannot enter into true, pure worship for anyone else, and we cannot bring anyone with us.

What if they don't come? What if they will not join us at His feet? Do we begin to "work" the people? Do we pull on their emotions? Do we sing the more emotional songs to help them find their way? Never! We must never "use" the anointing, or try and manipulate the anointing of God.

We are not manipulators of emotions, nor do we manipulate or use the power and presence of the Holy Spirit. So what do we do? We worship. That is all we are required to do, and that is all we are responsible to do. For the Lord is only seeking those who will worship Him. Whether anyone comes with us or not, is not our problem. That is completely up to them; all people will individually answer to the King of kings on judgment day as to how they approached Him while still remaining in these earth suits we call bodies.

It is not my job, my calling, or my gifting to lead others to worship the King in spirit and in truth. It is my calling as a worshiper to worship the King in spirit and in truth. While others watch, if they become hungry to come along, wonderful; if not, fine. I will go if no one follows. I will worship if I worship alone. Regardless of what others say or do; regardless of ridicule, mockery or judgment, I will worship. You are welcome to come with me. It will cost you everything. Make sure you are ready to pay the price. It will cost you… you. You are the price that is required to be a worshiper of the Lord. Give yourself, and you will receive back beyond any comparable imagination of rewards, compensation and remuneration. Don't play with Him. Don't pretend. You may fool the whole world while you lose your entire soul, but you will never fool Him. He knows your heart. He created you. He knows who you are, and He knows who you are not.

So be His bride, the One He is searching for over the whole earth… or don't be, but stop pretending. He deserves better than that. He would rather have no worship at all, than to have our performing, prideful, "all about us" worship. Pure worship. A pure worshiper. That is who He seeks. So choose. Which one are you?

Lord,

I give You

everything

that I am.

Chapter One Questions:

1. What is worship?

2. Who is worship?

3. What are we who worship required to be at His feet?

4. Who is the Lord seeking?

5. Are you ready to be found by Him?

6. How do I lead others to worship?

7. Where is our focus to be at all times during worship?

Chapter Two
Worship in Spirit

It makes sense that pure worshipers, those who seek only His face and nothing else, desire to worship Him in spirit and in truth, according to His Word. The truth we are speaking of here is a vital part of worship from a pure heart, and this chapter is dedicated to absorbing what it means to worship in spirit.

The word, "spirit" is in the *Strong's Concordance* and referenced as #7307. It is translated as the word, "ruach," pronunciation (roo-ach); it is defined as "spirit, wind, breath." This word occurs nearly 400 times.

Job 37:21
Even now men cannot look at the light when it is bright in the skies, when the wind has passed and cleared them.

Psalm 148:8
Fire and hail, snow and clouds; stormy wind, fulfilling His word...

Both of the above passages of scripture speak about "winds" related to storms. These are a type of "ruach."

Genesis 6:17, *And behold, I Myself am bringing floodwaters on the earth, to destroy from under heaven all flesh in which is the breath of life; everything that is on the earth shall die.*

Here we see "the ruach of life" is translated "the breath of life." Generally, "ruach" is translated "spirit," whether concerning the human spirit or a distressing spirit, as in I Samuel 16:23, *And so it was, whenever the spirit from God was upon Saul, that David would take a harp and play it with his hand. Then Saul would become refreshed and well, and the distressing spirit would depart from him.*

"Ruach" could also translate as "the Spirit of God." The Holy Spirit is especially presented in Isaiah as God puts His Spirit upon the Messiah. Isaiah 42:1, *Behold! My Servant whom I uphold, My Elect One in whom My soul delights! I have put My Spirit upon Him; He will bring forth justice to the Gentiles.*

He will pour out His Spirit upon Israel's descendants in Isaiah 44:3, *For I will pour water on him who is thirsty, and floods on the dry ground; I will pour My Spirit on your descendants, and My blessing on your offspring;* Yahweh and His Spirit both send the Anointed One, which is Jesus, in Isaiah 48:16, *Come near to Me, hear this: I have not spoken in secret from the beginning; from the time that it was, I was there. And now the Lord God and His Spirit have sent Me.* This is a reference to the triune God: Father, Son, and Holy Spirit.

> Pour Your Spirit on me, Lord!

The Spirit of God commissions and empowers the Messiah in Isaiah 61:1-3, *The Spirit of the Lord God is upon Me, because the Lord has anointed Me to preach good tidings to the poor; He has sent Me to heal the brokenhearted, to proclaim liberty to the captives, and the opening of the prison to those who are bound; to proclaim the acceptable year of the Lord, and the day of vengeance of our God; to comfort all who mourn, to console those who mourn in Zion, to give them beauty for ashes, the oil of joy for mourning, the garment of praise for the spirit of heaviness; that they may be called trees of righteousness, the planting of the Lord, that He may be glorified.* Much of this information comes from the Word Wealth section in the *Spirit-Filled Life Bible* concerning the actual word, "spirit."

In Philippians 3:3-4, *For we are the circumcision, who worship God in the Spirit, rejoice in Christ Jesus, and have no confidence in the flesh, though I also might have confidence in the flesh. If anyone else thinks he may have confidence in the flesh, I more so:*

Then in verse 10-11, *...that I may know Him and the power of His resurrection, and the fellowship of His sufferings, being conformed to His death, if, by any means, I may attain to the resurrection from the dead.*

...We are the circumcision, means those of us who have had our hearts "circumcised," paring away carnal ways in worship and doing away with dependence upon the flesh for salvation. So this phrase refers to those who are in Christ, fully committed and engrafted into His body. And if we are not dependent upon the flesh, this means that we are dependent upon the Spirit.

In the *Spirit-Filled Life Bible,* the following paragraph is from notes written concerning Philippians 3:3.

> The true sign of a right relation to God is not the observance of an external rite but a manifestation of the three characteristics mentioned. **Worship God in the Spirit** not only refers to one's being alive in the spirit (John 4:24) and thereby qualified for living worship, but also includes the Holy Spirit's enablement in expanded worship expressions: *in song* (Ephesians 5:18-19), *in prayer and singing* (I Corinthians 14:15), *and in communion with God* (I Corinthians 14:1-2).

John 4:24
God is Spirit, and those who worship Him must worship in spirit and truth.

Ephesians 5:18-19
And do not be drunk with wine in which is dissipation; but be filled with the Spirit, speaking to one another in psalms and hymns and spiritual songs, singing, and making melody in your heart to the Lord...

I Corinthians 14:15
What is the conclusion then? I will pray with the spirit, and I will also pray with the understanding. I will sing with the spirit, and I will also sing with the understanding.

I Corinthians 14:1-2
Pursue love, and desire spiritual gifts, but especially that you may prophesy. For he who speaks in a tongue does not speak to men but to God, for no one understands him; however, in the spirit he speaks mysteries.

These are outward manifestations that can be seen and heard in worship to God; but true worship is not even heard in the realm of the earth but more in the higher levels that human ears cannot hear. These are the sounds of the heart of a true worshiper to the heart of God on His throne. Without these worship sounds pouring forth from a worshiper who is willing to obey God and worship Him in spirit and truth, which are too high for human ears to hear with mental understanding, then there is only an observance, a ritual or religious 'sound' of worship.

> Even when
> I have no more
> words,
> I will praise
> You.

There are times when worship will not even be about audible sounds but the sounds of the reverberating spiritual heart making the movement of a broken reed coming up out of flesh, transcending the heavenlies, and then coming to rest in the throne room of God, at the feet of Jesus. These sounds may not be accessible to the human ear. They may be groanings which cannot be uttered, or sighs of an exhausted worshiper, whose battle to worship God is laid bare at His feet.

Romans 8:26-27
Likewise the Spirit also helps in our weaknesses. For we do not know what we should pray for as we ought, but the Spirit Himself makes intercession for us with groanings which cannot be uttered. Now He who searches the hearts knows what the mind of the Spirit is, because He makes intercession for the saints according to the will of God.

I heard the Lord say to me when I was searching for an explanation of how the Lord could call the death of those we love, precious, as in our case with our six year old daughter. He whispered this explanation to my heart.

> The earth is the womb of heaven. You are here to develop into who you will be for eternity. Once you are fully developed you are then birthed through the birthing canal that you call death, but I call life, into the realm of eternity. Here with Me in heaven, we all stand around the birth canal and once you enter in, all of heaven proclaims, "Oh, how precious!" That is why the scripture says in Psalm 116:15, *Precious in the sight of the Lord is the death of His saints.*

As I have meditated on this verse and this revelation by the Spirit of God to my spirit, I now understand this passage of scripture out of the *Message Bible* in Romans 8:18-26,

That's why I don't think there's any comparison between the present hard times and the coming good times. The created world itself can hardly wait for what's coming next. Everything in creation is being more or less held back. God reins it in until both creation and all the creatures are ready and can be released at the same moment into the glorious times ahead. Meanwhile, the joyful anticipation deepens.

All around us we observe a pregnant creation. The difficult times of pain throughout the world are simply birth pangs. But it's not only around us; it's within us. The Spirit of God is arousing us within. We're also feeling the birth pangs. These sterile and barren bodies of ours are yearning for full deliverance. That is why waiting does not diminish us, any more than waiting diminishes a pregnant mother. We are enlarged in the waiting. We, of course, don't see what is enlarging us. But the longer we wait, the larger we become, and the more joyful our expectancy.

Meanwhile, the moment we get tired in the waiting, God's Spirit is right alongside helping us along. If we don't know how or what to pray, it doesn't matter. He does our praying in and for us, making prayer out of our wordless sighs, our aching groans. He knows us far better than we know ourselves, knows our pregnant condition, and keeps us present before God. That's why we can be so sure that every detail in our lives of love for God is worked into something good.

The Lord is longing for those who will worship Him without the constraints of human sound waves that are understood by other humans. He is asking us to worship Him higher, ever calling us upward, to come to Him, kissing toward Him as we rise in the Spirit to the mighty King of kings, the very Lover of our soul. As we approach Him we are continually blowing kisses toward Him. *I am my beloved's and my beloved is mine*! Anything lower and less than this is done only for consumption of human pride, to elevate ones' own self, for the worshiper through his or her giftings to receive accolades from other mere humans. This is not worship at all, but performance. For what does it matter what other humans would think about your worship, if the King of kings and Lord of lords accepts it and longs for it! Worship God only!! Anything else drives us directly out of, "worship in spirit and truth," and into "worship in flesh." Yuck! The very sound of those words is so distasteful!

Fleshly, human performance is gone, over, and dead. When you look for it, you are only searching the cemetery for the old, dead things of human existence. Look for the living God. There you will find living and alive worship unto Him.

Will you say it with me?

"Holy, holy, holy,
Lord God Almighty,
Who was and is and is to come!"

In Revelation 4:8 we find, *The four living creatures, each having six wings, were full of eyes around and within. And they do not rest day or night, saying:*

> *"Holy, holy, holy,*
> *Lord God Almighty,*
> *Who was and is and is to come!"*

All at the same time, God is… past, present and future! God is past. God is present. God is future. Worship Him! Worship Him in spirit and in truth!

Spirit worship cannot be heard, or seen by humanity, therefore it cannot be praised either. True spirit worship is too high for human ears to hear, or human minds to understand. Spirit worship is heart to heart. The heart of man cries out to the heart of God, and He hears us! My heart is longing and searching for His heart. No longer do we look for those to "lead worship," once we realize the ridiculousness of that, for where has leading worship taken us? Certainly not to His feet too often!

We do not need those who lead us to worship! We need those who will worship Him in spirit and truth. These worshipers we can follow, not where they lead, but rather, we follow where they go. We go to His feet. Worship is individual purpose and personal choice. Even when worship happens within the ranks of multiple human beings it never stops being a personal choice, or an individual purpose. I will say that again. Corporate, congregational worship does not count as your worship or my worship! We can be swept up in tune (or not!) with a thousand other voices on Sunday morning and still be miles deep in the flesh! No, our Father, our Creator longs for spirit to Spirit communion with each of us. Can you feel Him drawing you by your spirit? Let Him in… worship Him, from your spirit. Worship Him in spirit and in truth.

"Holy, holy, holy,

Lord God Almighty,

Who *was* and *is* and *is to come!*"

Chapter Two Questions:

1. According to John 4:24, why must we worship God in spirit and truth?

____

____

____

____

____

____

2. True or False? It is necessary to have someone "lead worship" in order for true worship to take place.

____

____

____

____

____

____

3. True or False? Worship is about performance and sounding good to God.

____

____

____

____

____

____

4. How do I communicate with God when I am lost for words?

____

____

____

____

5. I Corinthians tells me that I am to desire __________ ______________ gifts. When I speak (pray, sing) in ____ ______________, God understands me and I speak mysteries.

6. Philippians 3, Paul indicates these three things that characterize believers:

1. They worship God __________________.
2. They rejoice in ____________________.
3. They have no ______________________ ______________________.

7. Spirit worship cries out… how?

____
____
____
____
____
____
____
____
____
____
____
____
____
____
____
____
____
____
____
____
____

Chapter Three
Worship in Truth

John 4:23
It's who you are and the way you live that count before God. Your worship must engage your spirit in the pursuit of truth. That's the kind of people the Father is out looking for: those who are simply and honestly themselves before him in their worship. God is sheer being itself - Spirit. Those who worship him must do it out of their very being, their spirits, their true selves, in adoration. (Message Bible)

When the Bible says He seeks those who worship Him in spirit and in truth then we must discover what "truth" really is. How can we worship the Lord in truth if we define truth only by our modern day society? In the *Message Bible* translation of John 4:23, we easily see that God is looking for people who are not pretending before Him. He is looking for people who are worshiping in reality of truth, nothing fake, or pretentious, or hidden.

> *We approach God in worship, through Jesus, who is the Way.*

Truth. This word has many perceived definitions in our English language. One could say that for some, truth is relative, not completely black and white. But from God's perspective truth is truth, and only truth. Jesus said in John 14:6, *I am the way, the truth, and the life.* So truth is Jesus. To truly worship the Lord in truth, we must worship the Lord in Jesus Christ! Jesus is truth, therefore we approach the throne of God in worship through Christ!

In the Greek language, "truth" is the word, "aletheia," which is pronounced (al-ay-thi-ah). In the *Strong's Concordance* it is #225. Aletheia is "the opposite of fictious, feigned, or false." It denotes "veracity, reality, sincerity, accuracy, integrity, truthfulness, dependability, and propriety."

Truth.

This word is used in a great quote from a famous movie. Jack Nicholson spoke the following words in "A Few Good Men," "You want the truth? You can't handle the truth!" Of course, we all know that God's truth and humanity's perception of truth may be quite different.

With God, truth is not merely a statement given to prove guilt or innocence, or to proclaim right or wrong. With God, truth is truth. God is truth. There is nothing in God that is not truth. **God is truth**. Wrap your mind around that statement and maybe we can grasp together what the Spirit of God is imparting to us through His Word. God's Word is truth, the whole truth, and nothing but the truth. In our legal society, we are asked to put our hand upon a Bible and swear in the courtroom to, "Tell the truth, the whole truth, and nothing but the truth." Truth is supposed to be able to determine the outcome and set apart emotional thoughts from reality.

In our society, we are filled with perceived ideas, concepts, and mental images of what truth really is. In the realm of the spirit may I introduce to you the very persona of truth? Truth held in flesh. Truth is not a *what.* Truth is *who.* When Moses asked God whom he should say had sent him, when the people and even Pharaoh would ask, God simply replied *"...I AM WHO I AM."* God said to Moses in Exodus 3:14, *Thus you shall say to the children of Israel, 'I AM has sent me to you.'* What a powerful truth! I AM is truth!

In the ancient Hebrew language the word "truth" is made up

of three symbols. The first two of these symbols spell the word, "mother." The three symbols for "truth" are positioned in the ancient language as the first symbol, the middle symbol, and the last symbol in the Hebrew alphabet. Even without seeing the symbols or even knowing the actual ancient Hebrew definition of this all-powerful ancient word, we can get the picture. Truth is the beginning, the middle, and the end of all things.

Jesus declared that He is the alpha and the omega, the beginning and the end. The spelling of the word "truth" is just that, the beginning letter and the end letter, plus the middle letter positioned in the middle of the word. So truth is all in all, beginning, middle and end; truth does not leave anything out. Truth covers the spectrum of all things, all colors, all meanings, nothing missing, nothing left out. Truth.

Here is the actual ancient definition for the word, "truth." "That which nurtures a covenant." Try to grasp this magnificent definition! Truth is that which nurtures (or mothers) the covenant. All else falls vastly short of anything worth pursuing. Truth will always nurture, watch over, take care of and mother a covenant.

What does that mean "to mother, or to nurture"? Can you see a mother hovering over a young child, or a newborn baby? Mothering God's way dispels all fear. Mothering God's way removes doubt, brings peace and rest. Mothering God's way causes the one who is being mothered to blossom and grow to full maturity. In this case, when truth is mothered God's way, it grows in our lives to full maturity. When truth is ever present in our lives, fear is pushed aside.

The word "fear" means "without mothering." "Mother" is defined as "strong water." So fear is in the life of the one who does not have strong water in their life. Since the Word of God is called the water of life, it is safe to say when one's life is filled with the Word of God daily, then fear cannot stay in that life. When the Bible is not a daily routine in one's life it is quite easy to see how fear can get in and stay in!

Our worship must be so vital to us, so important to our daily lives, that as a mother watches over and protects her child, so we protect and watch over our worship toward God. We will not take it for granted that we have the honor to worship the King. We protect it, in truth.

This is what our worship should be to God. He commands us to worship Him in truth, fully matured, God's way, which develops and births truth in our lives, our hearts and minds, our souls and spirits. When we walk in truth, then we can worship in truth. Let's say it this way. When we walk in Jesus, then we can worship the Father in Jesus!

Worshiping God in truth means that we are willing to apply the Word of God to our lives daily and expect the outcome of strong water to covenant our souls with Him. We want the truth; we receive the truth; we give back the truth through our worship at His feet.

Our world has many training places. We have schools, colleges and performing arts centers. We have dedicated, higher learning specialized universities to teach and train many professions. We have highly qualified people to impart to others the arts that have been attained. Even as I was growing up in Mississippi, specializing in piano and voice in my higher education, my greatest aspiration was to be accepted into the prestigious school of the arts in New York City, Julliard. The path was set and all went according to my human plans, but then God had other plans. I eventually won Miss America 1980 and the path shifted slightly. No matter how many different roads our lives take, I believe God is pleased with those of us who are willing to dream, have visions, make plans, but in the end, are most willing to give all our dreams and plans to Him and go where He tells us to go.

These types of specialty schools are prestigious, teaching and training in the realm of the arts, honing the gifts, and talents of performers to perform at their highest levels. But performance in itself is not the same as worship. Worship is not about gifts or talents. Worship is about the One who is being worshiped. Talents and gifts are given to humanity to use as instruments for the Spirit of God to move through us causing the sounds of His presence to fill us, captivate us, and escape from every opening of our humanity, filling the world in which we live with the very essence and sound of I AM! These sounds create within and without us the movement of a type of spirit and truth, a river, ever moving and flowing from the very depths of our soul, toward the throne of God. We can ride the waves of the supernatural sounds of God coming through us, ever beckoning us upward, all the way to His feet!

We are like great big woodwind instruments set in the midst of humanity. We are to have the ability to make sounds, music, worship, then with our yielded lives to the Spirit of God we give ourselves to God. We ask by our obedience for the Holy Spirit to blow through us making the eternal sounds of pure worship coming from within our being ever spiraling upward to the throne of grace. We yield our instruments to the breath of the Spirit of God. We become worship for His pleasure. We do not "do" worship. *We are worship!*

All the expressions, talents, and gifts given to humanity are to be given back to our Creator in pure worship. And yet, we don't teach those gifted with the ability how to give it back to God in purity of worship. We have not taught the responsibility and awesome privilege it is to be called to worship the King of kings. We have allowed the gifted and talented at times to pervert their gifts, whether it is singing, or playing an instrument, dancing, or drama. Most of this perversion of talent is not a conscious decision, but more of a subtle shift in focus, ever so slowly until one day we awaken, realizing our focus is skewed and completely off-center.

All these wonderful and most precious talents have been given to humanity for one purpose, to give back to the Lord of lords! But even in the church world we have subtly taught those with giftings to perform for the applause and accolades of humanity, receiving the pride of accomplishment into the very soul of the performer until the gift is so perverted that it can no longer be perceived from above as worship. It looks like the Tree of Knowledge, who was wrapped and entwined with the fallen worshiper himself, Lucifer.

From the view of heaven looking down upon created mankind, when our worship is more about the worshiper than about the One being worshiped, then there is not even the slightest resemblance to truth. In the Garden of Eden the only real truth was in the center of the garden, the Tree of Life. Who is the Tree of Life given to the center of the garden of God? Just a slight shift in focus and ones' eyes could move from the Tree of Life to the Tree of Knowledge.

Just a slight move of the head and our eyes can shift from one tree to the other, as they were both in the center of the garden. So if the Tree of Knowledge housed the fallen worshiper, Lucifer, now called Satan, then who stood right beside the Tree of Knowledge, housed and encased in the trunk and branches of the Tree of Life? Who was standing right in front of Adam and Eve every day, day in and day out, but never seen by either of them?

The Lord told us through His Word in Deuteronomy 30:19, *"I call heaven and earth as witnesses today against you, that I have set before you life and death, blessing and cursing; therefore choose life, that both you and your descendants may live; that you may love the Lord your God, that you may obey His voice, and that you may cling to Him, for He is your life and the length of your days; and that you may dwell in the land which the Lord swore to your fathers, to Abraham, Isaac, and Jacob, to give them."*

Lord, I will choose LIFE.

God set life and death before all of us, the blessing and the curse; and then He told us which one to choose. "Choose LIFE!" Of course, in the Garden of Eden, God would not set Lucifer as a choice before Adam and Eve and not also put the Lamb of God, the chosen One, Jesus Himself, Truth, Life, the Way, Blessing, also before them!

Eve stood right there and carried on conversations with the serpent wrapped up in the Tree of Knowledge, as Life in the form of a tree stood by watching. She never even saw Him. Who was there? Who was waiting to be chosen? Life was there; Truth was there; the Way was there. But Eve, nor Adam never saw Him standing there. Jesus stood ready and waiting in the midst of the garden of God. They didn't see Him. They didn't recognize Him. We have no time line as to how long these conversations went on between Lucifer and

Eve. It could have been weeks, months, even years. She never even noticed Jesus standing right beside her, trying to help her make the right choice.

When we begin to look upon our own needs, even those needs that seem so innocent, we are in grave danger of missing the truth. When we focus more on ourselves than the Lord God, our gifts, talents, and even callings can become our focus. We can easily get the truth mixed up with our own desires and this can cause us to become deceived, causing perversion within our own God-given talents. This perversion of gifts which were given to the earth for the worship of God can be so misused and misunderstood that the spirit of pride and perversion can take over. This yielding to soul/mind/will/emotional pride can so permeate the soul of the gifted that many times when I pray I can hear the Lord say, "I would rather have no worship than to have prideful worship." This must have been His words the moment Lucifer and one-third of the angels were kicked out of heaven. Can you hear the Father say, "I would rather have no worship as have prideful worship." For a period of time, we do not know how long, heaven was silent.

When my heart hears the heart of God say these words I immediately repent, for I know that I have grieved His heart so many times with my preconceived ideas of what worship really is. My heart breaks for my God who would do without His due worship because of the pride of humanity that is so desperate to fill the void of self-worth in our own existence. Instead of finally being completed while fulfilling the created purpose within each one of us to worship Him in spirit and in truth, we have allocated our deepest places of calling to worship Him to a few lines in a song, a few twirls of a dance, and a few thrill-seeking applause patterns of a drama.

To seek out the emotional thrill of making the spectator have chills or goose bumps has become the ultimate goal of every song, whether sung, played or danced. We must return to the fire of God and allow His presence to purify us once again and make us fit for the honor of worshiping Him.

There is no hiding who we are. There is no hiding our hearts from the One who knows us. As I said before, we may fool the entire world around us, but we can never fool our God! He knows us; He knows what I am thinking in my conscious mind, and He even knows the deepest thoughts of my subconscious mind!

Proverbs 16:2 states, *All the ways of a man are pure in his own eyes, but the Lord weighs the spirits.*

There is no place to hide from the eyes of the Lord. There are not enough places of my own pride to hide me from His sight. My own overdeveloped need for the approval of man cannot cast a big enough shadow for me to hide from the yearning pull of my Creator. He is calling me to "die to myself" and live to worship Him.

Matthew 5:8 says, *Blessed are the pure in heart for they shall see God.*

Pure in heart is a powerful position to be in with God. The more pure our hearts are, the more open our eyes become to be able to see HIM! The more pure we are with the Lord the closer we can get to His actual being. As His fire consumes the "flesh of us," we are left with more and more spirit. This is quite the spiritual equation; more spirit = less flesh. This is equality and balance God's way! Then as we approach Him in spirit and truth, we can come closer to Him. The closer we come in spirit and truth, the more we can worship Him. In our worship, to kiss toward Him, drawing nearer and nearer, blowing kisses toward Him, we continually and progressively position ourselves in His presence.

With God, the condition of our heart is much more important than the circumstances and situations surrounding our natural lives. Even our actions are not judged by the Lord without Him first examining our hearts and the motives that perpetuated such actions. So with God it is not as much about what we do, or what we don't do, but with what motive we do certain things, or even the motive of why we do not do certain things!

I ask you to examine your own heart before the Lord. I come before Him daily and I ask Him to allow me to see myself as I truly am, with all my faults and pride revealed. Why do I want to see myself this way? Because in His presence there is no guilt or condemnation. There is no fooling myself either. In His presence I can truly repent and ask Him without shame to help me be all about Him. He longs for us to repent, and believe Him. He longs for us to operate in the fullness of forgiveness. With a humble and broken heart we can pour forth His glorious praise without any thoughts of ourselves!

Psalm 19:12-14 states, *Who can understand his errors? Cleanse me from secret faults. Keep back Your servant also from presumptuous sins; Let them not have dominion over me. Then I shall be blameless, and I shall be innocent of great transgression. Let the words of my mouth and the meditation of my heart be acceptable in Your sight, O Lord, my strength and my Redeemer.*

I continually pray this Psalm before the Lord. It helps me to understand that I cannot "arrive" until I cross over from this earth into the heavens; but I can stay pure in the journey if I keep my eyes on Him, seeing God in all His glory!

Psalm 25:14-15 is another wonderful prayer to pray. *The secret of the Lord is with those who fear Him. And He will show them His covenant. My eyes are ever toward the Lord, for He shall pluck my feet out of the net.*

What net is that? The net of pride will try and hold you from moving further into His presence. But the Lord Himself, will pluck my feet out of that prideful net when I fear Him and keep my heart ever before Him. He will continue to show me His covenant, as I worship Him in spirit and in truth.

John 4:23

...Your worship must engage *your* spirit *in the* pursuit of truth. *That's the kind of people the* Father *is out looking for...*

(The Message Bible)

Chapter Three Questions:

1. The *Message Bible* says in John 4:23 that your worship must engage your spirit in the pursuit of ________________.

2. Who is *truth?*

____

____

____

____

____

____

____

____

3. God described Himself with what two powerful words in Exodus Chapter 3? ________________________________

4. The ancient Hebrew definition of the word "truth" is ______________________________.

5. What does this Hebrew definition mean to me today?

____

____

____

____

____

____

____

____

6. Worship is not about gifts and talents. It is about ____________________________________.

7. Talent has been given to humanity for one purpose, and that is ________________________________.

8. According to Matthew 5:8, what is promised to those who have a pure heart?

____

____

____

____

____

____

9. More ______________ = Less ______________

10. What being is responsible for worship becoming about performance, accolades and pride?

____

____

____

____

____

____

____

____

____

____

____

____

____

____

____

Chapter Four
Guard the Heart of Worship

Worshipers can be driven by their emotions. We must guard against this. In the Bible, many of the characters were worshipers. David wrote most of the Psalms in songs, poems, and spiritual songs. He was obviously very emotional. He had tremendous highs and his lows were to the depths of despair. As worshipers, we must guard our hearts and not be led by highs and lows of emotions. We must only be led by the Spirit of God and stay balanced and even within ourselves.

Discouragement and disappointment can be huge enemies in our pursuit of worship. We can even fall quickly into disobedience, rebellion, and stubbornness from the lying spirits of discouragement and disappointment! We have examples throughout the Bible of how these deceitful spirits can slip into a worshiper and how quickly focus can be lost, direction can be forgotten, and destiny can be consumed in the mountainous waves of discouragement and disappointment.

Help me guard my heart, oh Lord.

In I Kings 19:18, we find a conversation going on between Elijah and the Lord. Elijah was disappointed in the outcome of his most recent encounter. Elijah had obeyed the Lord and had confronted every false prophet, King Ahab and Queen Jezebel. He had been diligent to carry out the instructions of the Lord to the letter. He set up twelve stones for the twelve tribes of Israel, and built an altar in the name of the Lord. He dug a trench around it, put the wood on the altar, and then the bull on the wood. He filled four water pots with water and poured it on the burnt sacrifice and on the wood and then he repeated the saturating process with water a second and then a third time. The water completely saturated the offering, the wood, and filled the trench surrounding the altar. And after all this, Elijah waited. He waited on the Lord until it came to pass, at the time of the offering of the evening sacrifice that Elijah opened his mouth and declared to all listening, and to the Lord, "*Lord God of Abraham, Isaac, and Israel, let it be known this day that You are God in Israel and I am Your servant, and that I have done all these things at Your word. Hear me, O Lord, hear me, that this people may know that You are the Lord God, and that You have turned their hearts back to You again.*" (I Kings 18:36-37)

The fire fell straight out of heaven and it consumed the offering, the wood, the stones and dust. It even evaporated the water that was in the trench! God showed up for Elijah, and He showed Himself strong to all who were watching! After this event, Elijah and the people seized the prophets of Baal, and executed 450 of them.

Elijah told King Ahab, Queen Jezebel's husband, to eat and drink for there is the sound of the abundance of rain. Earlier Elijah had prophesied by the Lord to shut up heaven and there had not been any rain for three and a half years. The drought was hard on the land, and on the people.

God had continued to take care of His own; one hundred of God's prophets had been hidden from Jezebel, fifty in one cave and fifty in another cave, and the prophets had been sustained by the prophet Obadiah, with bread and water. These were very hard times for all the people. Elijah returned to present himself before Ahab and had followed the Lord's instructions to the letter. Elijah obeyed the voice of the Lord. Elijah called down fire from heaven. The fire had come down and had done what the prophets of Baal could not do. With the zeal of the Lord, Elijah had carried out vengeance upon the 450 false prophets. He killed them all!

Elijah had King Ahab's ear by this point, and when Elijah told the king to eat and drink in celebration as there is the sound of rain, the king believed God's prophet. Elijah went up to the top of Mount Carmel, and he bowed down to the ground and put his face between his knees in a worshiping position to the Lord. He spoke to his servant and told him to go take a look at the sky above the sea and report back to him what he saw.

When his servant came back he reported to the prophet Elijah that he saw nothing. Elijah sent him to look again and again, and each time he came back and said that he had seen nothing. But on the seventh time he reported that he saw a cloud rising out of the sea the size of a man's hand. When Elijah heard about the small cloud rising, he told his servant to tell King Ahab to prepare his chariot and go down the mountain so the king would not get caught in the downpour of rain that was about to come upon them.

While the servant of Elijah went to report to the king to hurry up, the sky became black with clouds and wind and very heavy rain began to pour down upon them. Then the hand of the Lord came upon Elijah, and strengthened him, and he ran so fast that he passed King Ahab in his chariot, and reached the entrance of Jezreel before the king!

Once King Ahab got to his queen, Jezebel, he began to tell her all the events that had taken place. He told her about the prophet Elijah calling forth the rain that had ended the drought and also how Elijah had executed all 'her' false prophets. Instead of Jezebel having a change of heart toward God, and believing in the God of Elijah who had ended the 3 ½ year drought, she was angrier than ever. She declared to Elijah, *"So let the gods do to me, and more also, if I do not make your life as the life of one of them by tomorrow about this time."*

This must have come as quite a shock to Elijah! His next reaction gives us an idea of what he must have been thinking and expecting from Jezebel. Obviously, her reaction was not what he expected! Instead of her giving in at this point, and confessing that Elijah's God is the only true God, Jezebel became even angrier, and made a threat to kill Elijah within 24 hours! The very next verse tells us Elijah's reaction to her threats. It says in I Kings 19:3, *he arose and ran for his life....*

This has always puzzled me as to why Elijah would run for his life. He had just witnessed the power of God to pour fire down from heaven, burning up the sacrifice, the altar, and even all the water. He had the faith and the strength along with the people who joined him to execute 450 false prophets. He had believed God over and over again in prayer until God sent the down pouring rain after a three and a half year drought. He had been so empowered by the Holy Spirit in his physical body that he outran the king's chariot pulled by a fast-racing horse! And yet, in the face of one hate-filled woman's threatening words, he ran for his life!! What happened to his faith? What happened to this powerful warrior prophet for God?

Elijah had seen some of the most poignant events in history at the hand of the Lord and yet one horribly mean woman's words caused him to run for his life. Why? I believe Elijah had allowed himself to have his own human expectations of the outcome of these events, instead of allowing the Lord to set his expectations. Elijah had obviously expected Jezebel to turn toward God once King Ahab told her what he had witnessed God doing. He must have anticipated her turning all her evil affections over to the Lord and he must have fully expected her heart to be changed. She was not changed, and Elijah was disappointed... not just disappointed, but devastated.

We must not become empowered by our own expectations and forget to stay focused on the Lord! No matter what the outcome of certain events in our lives we must not be moved. It is best to wear spiritual blinders when possible, and not get caught in thought! What do I mean? "Lord, I thought You were going to do so and so! Lord, I thought they would do so and so! Lord, I thought…" on and on we can go in this merry-go-round of thought until our minds are caught! Don't get caught in thought! Stay focused on the Lord at all times.

He ran for his life into the wilderness, left his servant at Beersheba, and went another day's journey deeper into the wilderness and finally collapsed beneath a juniper tree. There he prayed for his life to be over and he said to God, "It is enough! Now, Lord, take my life, for I am no better than my fathers!"

Elijah had set himself up for a fall by having expectations set up by his own mind instead of following the leading of the Holy Spirit. He lay down under the tree and slept and an angel touched him; the angel told him to arise, eat, and drink some water. Then he lay down again and slept. The angel of the Lord came a second time and touched him. The angel told him to get up and eat because the journey had been too great for him.

So Elijah got up and ate and drank, and the sustenance given by the angel of the Lord provided strength for him for forty days and nights as he traveled all the way to Horeb, the mountain of God. At this point, Elijah went into a cave and spent the night there. The word of the Lord came to Elijah and God said to him, *"What are you doing here, Elijah?"*
(I Kings 19:9)

Elijah answered the Lord by saying, *"I have been very*

zealous for the Lord God of hosts; for the children of Israel have forsaken Your covenant, torn down Your altars, and killed Your prophets with the sword. I alone am left; and they seek to take my life." (I Kings 19:10)

In verses 11-19 the Lord said, "*Go out, and stand on the mountain before the Lord." And behold, the Lord passed by, and a great and strong wind tore into the mountains and broke the rocks in pieces before the Lord, but the Lord was not in the wind; and after the wind an earthquake, but the Lord was not in the earthquake; and after the earthquake a fire, but the Lord was not in the fire; and after the fire a still small voice.*

So it was, when Elijah heard it, that he wrapped his face in his mantle and went out and stood in the entrance of the cave. Suddenly a voice came to him, and said, "What are you doing here, Elijah?" And he said, "I have been very zealous for the Lord God of hosts; because the children of Israel have forsaken Your covenant, torn down Your altars, and killed Your prophets with the sword. I alone am left; and they seek to take my life."

Then the Lord said to him; "Go, return on your way to the Wilderness of Damascus; and when you arrive, anoint Hazael as king over Syria. Also you shall anoint Jehu the son of Nimshi as king over Israel. And Elisha the son of Shaphat of Abel Meholah you shall anoint as prophet in your place. It shall be that whoever escapes the sword of Hazael, Jehu will kill; and whoever escapes the sword of Jehu, Elisha will kill. Yet I have reserved seven thousand in Israel, all whose knees have not bowed to Baal, and every mouth that has not kissed him."

So he departed from there, and found Elisha the son of Shaphat, who was plowing with the twelve yoke of oxen before him, and he was with the twelfth. Then Elijah passed by him and threw his mantel on him.

Why am I telling this story and how does it relate to worship? Worship is about relationship between God and mankind. Elijah was called and appointed by God as His prophet. Elijah was God's man for the nation. The more Elijah saw God do to prove who He is, would you not expect him to become more and more dependent upon the Lord God?

That is what I would expect, yes. But it seems the more familiar Elijah became with the power of God, the more Elijah began to have his own mental expectations of the outcome of certain events. We must be careful to protect our hearts and minds from our own expectations. We must stay in tune with the Spirit of God and His leading so we do not set up our own ideas, thoughts, and outcomes of events where God is leading.

The more I have meditated on this story before the throne of God the more I see certain warnings by the Spirit of God to my own heart and mind. First of all, we must follow the Lord. We must not lead the Lord. Elijah was following the Lord right up to the point where he "ran for his life." Once he began to be self-preserving, instead of trusting the Lord, his future and his usefulness to God as a prophet was over in God's kingdom.

Elijah obviously thought that once Jezebel heard the news that the drought was over, and that Elijah had a big hand in bringing this to pass, he must have expected her to turn to him and embrace him, or at the very least, see that his God is the one true God. But she did not see it that way at all. In fact, the more God did to prove Himself as God, the madder Jezebel became! She became so mad that she threatened

Elijah's life and even after all he had witnessed as the power of God, instead of Elijah standing his ground with this wicked woman, he fled for his life! We must learn to obey God without ever having to have any knowledge of the outcome of our obedience.

So Elijah was disappointed for sure. His expectations of what God would do were not fulfilled. He got into his flesh and began to fear for his life. He ran away, and he did what many worshipers do in times of trouble; he isolated himself away from even his servant. He left his servant behind and traveled even further into the wilderness of his disappointment and depression as he pulled away from the people he trusted most.

Disappointment, depression and isolation can lead to a deep pit of exhaustion. He became so exhausted (trying to make God do what we expect, want, and think we need, is so exhausting!) that he fell down under a tree and went into a deep, exhausted sleep. But God being the God that He is, sent an angel to speak to him, feed him, give him water, and strengthen him. But Elijah the prophet was more focused on his own expectations rather than on God. Even after God sent an angel to awaken and strengthen him, he fell back into exhausted sleep.

Again, God being the God that He is, had the angel touch Elijah, awaken him, feed, water, and strengthen him again! Now this was not any ordinary food, water, or strength. This was high-powered stuff! So powerful with nutrition was this food, water and strength that Elijah survived with this "super-powered soul food" for forty days and nights! No matter how much Elijah was disappointed in God, no matter how exhausted Elijah had let himself become, God never left him. God stayed with him, and continued to speak and direct him. He directed Elijah where to go, and then God met him there. The first thing God asked Elijah was, *"What are you doing here, Elijah?"*

Now why would God ask Elijah such a question when He had been the very One who had instructed Elijah to come to that very place!? I don't believe God was asking Elijah why was he in that particular location as much as God was asking Elijah what he was doing in such a mental/emotional place as this. I believe that God was saying to Elijah that he should not be in this place of thought, disappointment, discouragement, etc. But Elijah being so self-focused by this point missed the target of the question and his answer was all about himself.

First Elijah began to rehearse to the Lord what all he had done for Him. "You know me God. You know I am very zealous for You." Then in typical human fashion Elijah began to blame others for this state he was in. *"...the children of Israel have forsaken Your covenant, torn down Your altars, and killed Your prophets with the sword."* Elijah must have known this was not news to the Lord. The Lord knows all things even before they actually take place in this earth realm, but Elijah felt it necessary to rehearse these blaming choices to God. And then he went on to completely seal the deal of where his heart truly was when he said, *"And I alone am left; and they seek to take my life."*

Standing before God Almighty, King of kings and Lord of lords, he must have been completely out of it, to take such a prideful stand before God! To speak to the Lord as if He does not know the truth... wow!!!! I am amazed... and yet, even as I write these words, my own heart condemns me of similar conversations I have had with the Lord. When even our prayers reflect to the Lord our self-focused hearts, we are on extremely dangerous ground with Him.

The Lord is patient and He is kind for, at this point, He did not continue on in conversation but took the opportunity to *show* Elijah who He really IS! God told Elijah to go out and stand on the mountain before Him, and the Lord passed by. In His passing a huge wind tore into the mountains and broke the rocks into pieces. But the Lord was not in the wind. Then the Lord sent an earthquake but the Lord was not in the earthquake. Then the Lord sent a fire to follow up the wind and earthquake but the Lord was not in the fire either. After all this big show the Lord put on for Elijah, the Lord spoke to him in a *"still small voice."*

Can you imagine how Elijah must have felt at this very moment? Can you imagine how he must have been shaking in his sandals!? But Elijah wrapped his face in his mantel and went out and stood in the entrance of the cave. As he stood there, the Lord God asked him the same question He had asked him earlier… the exact same question!!!! *"What are you doing here, Elijah?"*

I have come to learn when God does not change the question to me, I must learn to change the answer I give Him. But Elijah did not change his answer, which told the truth of his heart toward God. When our answer to God's questions do not change, and we continue to defend ourselves before the throne of God - when our focus is still on ourselves instead of on Him and Him alone, then we must be ready for the consequences of our heart choices. Elijah was a great prophet for God as long as God stayed at the center of his worship and the center of his heart, but once he became self-focused and his answers to God always sounded like, "What about me, what about me, what about me?" then God moved on. Then God moved on! Just think about it! Do we ever want God to "move on" in our lives and leave us behind in our pitiful, self-focused condition? I do not! Please Lord, stay with me and help me get over myself!

The next directions God spoke to Elijah were to finish up this earth realm, appoint his successor, go get him and train him. His successor was Elisha. We must not become so self-focused in what we "do" for the Lord that it becomes in any way about us. When it does, we are finished and our successor has already been appointed and is on the way to replace us before the King.

Elijah was a great man of God, as long as his heart stayed purely focused on God. *Blessed are the pure in heart, for they shall see God.* (Matthew 5:8) As long as what we see is God, this reflects the purity of our hearts. But when we stop seeing God, and we see ourselves, then this reflects the impurity of our hearts, and we shall not see God any longer. A pure heart is essential to stay in worship. It has never been and it never will be about me, or you. It has always been, and it always will be about HIM. We must worship Him in spirit and in truth… pure spirit and pure truth, nothing less.

God is purifying His called and appointed worshipers even now as I write this. He is coming for a purified bride, who is a purified worshiper. The bride of Christ is not a separate entity to the worshiper. They are one and the same. His purified bride will worship Him in spirit and in truth.

Psalm 51:10-13 is a wonderful prayer that David prayed. It has become one of my favorites to pray in helping me keep my pride broken before Him.

Create in me a clean heart, O God, and renew a steadfast spirit within me. Do not cast me away from Your presence, and do not take Your Holy Spirit from me. Restore to me the joy of Your salvation, and uphold me by Your generous Spirit. Then I will teach transgressors Your ways, and sinners shall be converted to You.

As worshipers, *we must guard our hearts* and not be led by highs *and* lows *of emotions.* We must only be led by the Spirit of God and stay *balanced* and *even* within ourselves.

Chapter Four Questions:

1. __________________ and ____________________ can be huge enemies in our pursuit of worship.

2. We cannot be led by emotion - we must be led by the

_____________________ _________ _______________.

3. Worship is about ____________________ between God and mankind.

4. What happened to Elijah when his human expectations got in the way of his trust in God?

____

____

____

____

____

____

____

5. In relation to Elijah's story, name one thing that can put us on dangerous ground with the Lord.

____

____

____

____

____

____

____

____

____

____

____

____

6. What did God ultimately do when Elijah became self-focused?

____

____

____

____

____

____

____

____

7. Seeing God reflects the _______________ of our hearts. Seeing ourselves reflects the _____________ of our hearts.

8. In relation to this chapter, what is essential to stay in worship?

____

____

____

____

____

____

____

____

9. Name four things that we must guard against in order to maintain pure hearts of worship:

1.

2.

3.

4.

Chapter Five
A Prepared Worshiper

Matthew 25:1-13
Then the kingdom of heaven shall be likened to ten virgins who took their lamps and went out to meet the bridegroom. Now five of them were wise, and five were foolish. Those who were foolish took their lamps and took no oil with them, but the wise took oil in their vessels with their lamps. But while the bridegroom was delayed, they all slumbered and slept. And at midnight a cry was heard: 'Behold, the bridegroom is coming; go out to meet him!' Then all those virgins arose and trimmed their lamps. And the foolish said to the wise, "Give us some of your oil, for our lamps are going out." But the wise answered, saying, "No, lest there should not be enough for us and you; but go rather to those who sell, and buy for yourselves." And while they went to buy, the bridegroom came, and those who were ready went in with him to the wedding, and the door was shut. Afterward the other virgins came also, saying, "Lord, Lord, open to us!" But he answered and said, "Assuredly, I say to you, I do not know you." Watch therefore, for you know neither the day nor the hour in which the Son of Man is coming.

> *Lord, I watch and wait for You.*

We are living in a season when we need to be *watching*. Jesus, the Bridegroom is coming for His ready bride. We do not know the day or the hour, but we know He is coming. Then why do we allow our own flesh to dictate our many self-willed and sin-perpetuating actions? We must not be like the five foolish virgins, and yet, when I take a good look at my own life, I see many permissive things that I have allowed to stay in and on me. These issues, left unconfronted could have caused me to be found not ready had He come at any time before now. If you are honest with yourself as I am being with myself, you may find those untrimmed areas in your life: spirit, soul, and flesh, also.

I am a country girl, from the hills of Mississippi. I grew up knowing what it was like to lose electric power for periods of time. We used to have kerosene lamps, which when I read this passage of scripture from Matthew 25, makes me think back to those days. When a lamp or a candle has a wick, and it is not trimmed properly, when lit, the untrimmed area can cause a great deal of smoke, but not much light. Smoke in itself can create a camouflage; it can actually hide the light, causing the term most of us are very familiar with, a smoke screen! In our own worship, we must be careful to come before Him with the wicks of our lives trimmed.

In the Word Wealth section of the *Spirit-Filled Life Bible* at Matthew 25, the word "trimmed" is highlighted and discussed. "Trimmed" in the *Strong's Concordance* is #2885 and it is the Greek word "kosmeo," pronounced (kos-meh-oh). We can compare this word to a more familiar word in our English language, "cosmetic" which means "to beautify, arrange, decorate, furnish, embellish, adorn, and put in order." Here we can draw the conclusion from this one word used in context of this passage of scripture that this is a warning to the bride of Christ that we are to make ourselves ready, to watch and get ourselves in proper position, and relationship. We are to beautify, arrange, decorate, furnish, embellish, adorn, and put ourselves in order for His coming.

But let's think of this action of trimming. When we trim a piece of fabric, we cut away what is not needed. When we trim a pencil of the unwanted wood around the lead, we expose what we need in order to write. When we trim the wicks in our lamps of life, we are to cut away those areas in which smoke is produced instead of fire and light! God is telling us if we want to be found ready and worthy we must trim away the dead portions of our lives that do not produce any semblance of His image.

As we talked about in Chapter Two, this is a type of spiritual, emotional, mental and soul realm *circumcision.* We are required as His being-made-ready-bride to keep our own wicks trimmed, and our own lamps filled with enough oil. This is not the duty or responsibility of someone else in our lives. This is my sole responsibility! I must keep my own lamp filled with enough oil to sustain me for the immediate need and for the long range, undetermined time it will take until He comes for me. I must continually keep the burned portions of my flesh, mind, will, emotions, and spirit trimmed and cut away, as a type of spiritual circumcision, causing only life to be produced in my daily walk with Him.

The numbers in this story are very significant to the unfolding dramatic meaning of this story that surpasses a moment in history. This beautiful, long-awaited story is a picture of our future; it is the unfolding drama of the waiting bride for the coming of the Bridegroom to take her away with Him. We are His bride and we wait for Him, our soon coming King, even now. We wait. While we wait, we who worship are allowing the fire of His presence to burn within us, causing the fire of His presence to purify us, making us more like Him, and less like our old, unregenerate selves.

God is the all-consuming fire that brings about our purification, and the time spent is what it takes to cause us to be more like Him with each passing day. But there will come a day, and I pray it is soon, when the midnight cry will sound, and it will be heard, "Behold, the bridegroom is coming! Go out to meet Him!"

The first significant number is "ten." This powerful number has many dimensional meanings and I could spend days writing about these amazing connections that prove the all-powerful vertical directions of our God and His bride. Ten means "testimony." This story is one of the brides testifying for the Bridegroom! The bride is waiting. While she waits, she gives her testimony of how she met Him, how she loves Him. She shares with all whom she meets, the power of His love for her, and her undying love for Him. She shares the testimony of how they met, and how they fell in love. She can never stop talking about Him, because He is the very lover of her eternal soul, and because of Him, she is eternal.

Ten is also the number that defines the law of God. Once we start talking about the laws of God it is hard to find a place to stop! When we think about the word "law," many times we miss the beauty of it, and only think of the harshness of the word. But laws are more than for punishment. Laws are for protection. Yes, we know the law of God's judgment, but we must remember the law of His love! We know the ten laws given to the children of Israel under the leadership of Moses, but that was not God's idea! He wanted the Israelites to trust Him completely and live with Him in relationship! But the people demanded rules and laws to live by. God's law of love and forgiveness was ever reaching toward them even then, but they demanded rules, thus the Ten Commandments were given.

The number ten also means "responsibility." God's best for all of humanity is to live in deep and divine relationship with Him, but most of the time, we foolishly ask for rules, laws and lines to fence us in. Why would we do this? Because we don't trust ourselves! And we certainly don't trust our God! If we could learn to trust Him, then we can learn to live in the intimacy of responsible love. Lord, I trust You because I choose to trust You; therein lies the power of that trust.

There are ten commandments, and there were ten plagues. There were ten patriarchs before the flood of Noah's time in Genesis 5. When Abraham was negotiating with God over Sodom and Gomorrah, he prayed for ten righteous people to be found. Abraham was looking for a testimony for God through the number ten to use but ten righteous people were not found. In the passage of scripture used here in Matthew 25, ten is the number needed to give legality under the Jewish law to have a function or a wedding. In Luke 19, we find the ten servants entrusted with ten pounds, and the one servant was rewarded with the authority over ten cities.

In Romans 8:38, we can easily see the love of God, His law of love, conquers ten powers: 1. Death 2. Life 3. Angels 4. Principalities 5. Powers 6. Things present 7. Things to come 8. Height 9. Depth 10. Any other creature. None of these shall be able to separate us from the love of God! God's law of love is above and beyond any and all things!

The tithe is the tenth of the whole of our income. So when we "cut it off" from ourselves and give it back to God, then the tithe becomes the circumcised part of our finances. When we keep that first tenth part of the whole of our income, we are keeping that portion which belongs to the Lord. Like the natural part of physical circumcision, it has been proven through medical science that when we keep that portion of flesh that should be cut off, it can cause sickness and disease later on in the physical flesh.

When we keep the portion of our income that has been designated as the tithe it is not about the money at all! It is about the element of intimacy with the Father God. He is asking us to trust Him beyond our own ability to provide for ourselves. He is asking us to trust Him with the circumcised portion. He is simply saying, "Give it to Me. Will you trust Me with it?" Tithing is intimacy on a monetary level. When a person who is in a position of worship cannot trust God to take care of them, provide for them, then they can never be trusted to go into the most intimate place of His presence and simply worship Him without fear!

Ten means "the whole being, the entire." So when ten is the number used for the virgins who are waiting for the return of the Bridegroom, it is referring to the entire bride of Christ who is waiting for His return. How do we become His bride? We say, "Yes" when the question is asked, "Will you marry Me?"

So in this story we find the "ten," or the whole bride of Christ anxiously waiting for His return. But He does not come quickly, and they wait, wait, and wait. Saying yes to the question of, "Will you marry Me?" is a very important response, but the answering of the question correctly is no more important than the "how we wait" criteria. So He, our Bridegroom has asked the question, "Will you marry Me?" and we have answered, "Yes!" Now the question is from the throne of God, "Will you wait for Me?" and we enthusiastically answer, "Yes! We will wait for You!"

In the beginning we do wait, patiently… we wait. But while they waited, while the Bridegroom delayed they all slumbered and slept. There is no use trying to deny it. The Bible is true; it cannot be refuted. At one time or another any and all of us as His bride have drifted off to sleep and some are still asleep even now! We must awake, oh sleeping bride! We must arise and prepare to meet Him! He is coming! Wake up! Get up! Get ready!

The Bible says that while they were sleeping and slumbering the cry was heard that He is coming! There is no doubt that right now the church; Christ's bride is fast asleep! We should get ready because while we are sleeping, is when the shout will be heard!

I feel as if the Lord has called upon me to be the cry of His coming! Are you sleeping? Can you hear me calling you? Get up, and trim your lamps, check your oil levels and get ready!

But like all stories there is always a twist, a turn, an unexpected event that causes a stir. In this story, we have five virgins who were foolish and five who were wise. And like all society today, we have those who have not saved, or lived moderately, but have been foolish, demanding that the "haves" give to the "have-nots." All the way back to when the Bible was written after Jesus was crucified we have been told that five wise people cannot save enough to have a future for themselves and the foolish also. Living righteously before God is personal; it is one on One! The five who saved enough oil and who kept their lamps trimmed could not be "good enough" for themselves and for those who did not save their oil, or buy enough oil, or keep their wicks trimmed.

I stand before God and I answer for what I have done, and for what I have not done. I alone am responsible for the choices that I have made. I alone must answer for my decisions and my life. I ask the Lord daily to show me those areas in my life where I need to trim the wick of foolishness. I ask the Lord to show me where I can buy more "oil" of the Spirit of God. What do I use to pay for this oil? I give myself; if I keep my "self," it is worth nothing! But when I give myself to the Lord He causes me to be worth what He has paid for me; He paid for me with His blood, therefore my person is worth enough to buy much oil of the Spirit! I have enough to purchase what is necessary to keep my oil filled, my lamp lit, and my wick trimmed! But I don't have enough for you. Only you hold the key to your purchase, you have yourself to give back to Him!

"Five" is also a very important number as it means "grace." It is only by His grace that any of us could ever be found ready for His coming. His grace is sufficient for me. His grace is sufficient for you! Five virgins were not ready. They heard the cry, and they jumped up, and started making preparations for His coming, but it was too late. They tried to beg the five wise virgins who had enough oil, and had kept their wicks trimmed, for help, but like all responsible things of this earth, it is a one man show. Each virgin was responsible for her own preparations, timing, and readiness. The five who were not ready had to leave the "waiting place," and go out and try to find enough oil to purchase.

I can just imagine the scene now. The five foolish ones were running down the streets, trying to get their wedding gowns on, doing their hair, nails, shaving, grooming, flossing! They must have been frantic, knowing that while they should have been staying prepared, they had slept instead. Since they were foolish, they most probably were blaming each other asking, "Why didn't you wake me? Why didn't you help me? Why didn't you…" It was too late. There was no one to blame. They found oil to buy, probably had to pay way too much for it, and most probably cut more wick than was needed which is what happens when you are using a knife to cut away the old, while running frantically down the street! But they finally thought they were prepared and ran all the way back to the waiting place.

When they arrived at the door, it was already shut. The Bridegroom had come and found the five wise virgins waiting at the waiting place. He took them in His arms and they went inside. The door was shut… forever. The five foolish virgins came running back shouting, yelling, and banging on the door that was shut. "Let us in, let us in, we are ready now! Open the door! Please!!!"

But it was too late. The Bridegroom had come and had taken those from the waiting place who were prepared and had stayed ready. When He found five with enough oil of the spirit, and all the burned wick of the flesh had been trimmed away, He took those and closed the door behind Him.

He heard the foolish ones at the door. I can just imagine the tears in His just and righteous eyes, as He comforted and quieted those five wise virgins whom He had found ready. As He slipped away from their firm grasp on His hand; He leaned His head gently against the already closed door. He felt the reverberation of the sound waves coming through the wood of the door, as the foolish virgins pounded and begged. Can you see those who had put off their preparations? With tears and sobs of knowing their foolishness, they cried for Him to open the door. As much as He longed to give them more time, He knew that He could not. The time had been set by His all-knowing Father.

Only the Father knew when the Bridegroom must come. Only the Father knew those who were ready and waiting in the waiting place. Only the Father knew that no matter how much time you gave to the foolish virgins, they would never be found ready and waiting in the waiting place. They could only be found sleeping and slumbering in the waiting place.

With the finality of the words of the Bridegroom spoken, as the foolish virgins cried out, "We are ready now, we know You. We know Your name. We have done many things in Your name. Lord, Lord, open the door to us! We know You!!!!"

The Bridegroom leaned His head on the door, and with His tender hand pressed up against it, He simply said, "I am certain of this one thing and I say it to you to hear with My voice. I do not know you." It is finished. It is over. It is done.

Five virgins were ready. That's fifty percent of the body of Christ will be found ready. That is a percentage that cannot be changed, as it is written in God's Word. Therefore, we must not even be at the fifty percent mark yet, because if fifty percent of the bride of Christ were ready, He would have come by now! Oh, my heart hurts even to write this, but it must be true, as His word is true. We are not ready, oh, sleeping bride. Awake from your slumber, awake from your sleep! Arise, and make ready for He is coming!

Which one are you? Are your preparations done, or do you always need "just a little more time?" Are you in the waiting place, worshiping Him while you wait? Or are you sleeping? You know for sure. But more importantly, He knows. You may know Him, but does He know you? You may know His name, but does He know your name? You may call Him by name, but does He call you by name?

> Lord!
> *I long to be* ready *when You return*
> *for Your Bride!*
> *Help me to* become *and to*
> remain
> *a* prepared *worshiper.*

Chapter Five Questions:

1. We are living in a season when we need to be ____________________.

2. To be found ready at the Bridegroom's return, we must have trimmed away all things that …

____

____

____

____

____

____

____

____

3. Based on the story of the five virgins, what percentage of the body of Christ will not be found ready at His return?

____

____

____

____

____

____

____

____

____

4. This trimming process is a type of spiritual, emotional, mental and soul realm ____________________.

5. God's first choice was for us to trust Him and live with Him by ________________, not laws.

6. How can we "purchase" the oil to keep our lamps full? What does God require of us for this transaction?

____

____

____

____

____

____

____

____

____

____

____

____

7. How can I keep my heart and life prepared for His coming?

____

____

____

____

____

____

____

____

____

____

Chapter Six
A Praying Worshiper

Psalm 46:10
Be still and know that I am God.

Notice in the above scripture that the Lord calls Himself, I AM. Be still and know that I AM. When we have our minds fixed on anything other than who He is, we are in turmoil and trouble. He is… what more do we need to know?

Be still and rest in Him. Be still and understand, conceive the answer is Jesus. Stop trying to come up with another way other than trusting in Him. You can spend a lifetime of useless looking around for other ways of escape, only to find there are no other exits except Him, our Lord, Savior, and King of kings.

Stop fidgeting in the flesh. Stop fidgeting in the soul and spirit. Be still and meditate on Him. Listen more, talk less in prayer. Seek the Lord while He may be found.

Don't come into His presence to simply receive; come to worship, to stand in the gap, to allow the Holy Spirit to pour through you toward the throne of God. If there is anything on your mind other than the Lord, whether your mind is on how you look, sound, etc., whether it is on the pastor, staff, those standing around you, if they are pleased, what they are thinking, if your mind is on the people in the audience, the other musicians, the cameraman, your hands, your voice, your hair, if your focus is anywhere other than the Lord then you are not worshiping. Worshipers are created to worship! If you are doing anything other than worshiping, then you are not worshiping! You are wasting your time, and most importantly you are wasting God's time.

Go do something else. Worship is not about *doing* it anyway. Worship is about *being* it. *We are to be worship, not do worship.* Our services have been filled with generations of people *doing* worship. God is not pleased. He is looking, searching the whole earth over for those who are *being* worship. His eyes are making rapid movements back and forth looking for someone who will be willing to only worship Him in spirit and in truth.

That is why we prepare ourselves, our appearance, our attitudes, our abilities, skills, and talents, all preparation necessary for excellence in His presence, before we enter a service, meeting, or gathering to worship. We are to have used prior preparation in all things that could distract us. There should be no "flying by the seat of our pants" in the presence of Almighty God. This does not exclude spontaneous worship, no! God longs for spontaneous worship that flows unhindered, out of our adoration-filled hearts, pouring forth to Him. In regards to preparation for worship though, the most important thing is prayer, prayer, prayer!

Isaiah 6:1-8
In the year that King Uzziah died, I saw the Lord sitting on a throne, high and lifted up, and the train of His robe filled the temple. Above it stood seraphim; each one had six wings: with two he covered his face, with two he covered his feet, and with two he flew. And one cried to another and said: "Holy, holy, holy is the Lord of hosts; the whole earth is full of His glory!"

And the posts of the door were shaken by the voice of him who cried out, and the house was filled with smoke. So I said: "Woe is me, for I am undone! Because I am a man of unclean lips, and I dwell in the midst of a people of unclean lips; for my eyes have seen the King, the Lord of hosts."

Then one of the seraphim flew to me, having in his hand a live coal which he had taken with the tongs from the altar, and he touched my mouth with it, and said: "Behold, this has touched your lips; your iniquity is taken away, and your sin purged." Also I heard the voice of the Lord, saying: "Whom shall I send, and who will go for Us?" Then I said, "Here am I! Send me."

Isaiah was "undone" in the presence of Almighty God. God's presence was there and filled the temple; worship was already in progress as seraphim angels were circling the throne crying to one another, *"Holy, holy, holy is the Lord God Almighty!"*

Their cries could have been translated as "Pure, pure, pure!" The word "seraphim" means "fiery creatures." These are creatures on fire, encircling and crying out to God: Father, Son, and Holy Spirit! These fiery worshipers are an example to us as to how we are to worship. We are to be spiritually on fire in our worship. What does this fire represent? Purity in our worship must be found! Once Isaiah witnessed this kind of pure worship it caused him to fall down on his face before the Lord, recognizing his need for the fire of God in his life to bring purification. When the presence of God does not cause us to want to repent, to want to fall on our faces, to want to ask Him to make us holy even as He is holy, then our hearts are not prepared or ready to be in His presence.

Prerequisites of a worshiper…

A worshiper must:
be saved.
be filled with the Holy Spirit.
be surrendered to His presence.
be crucified with Christ.
be reconciled to God.

be holy.
be righteous.
be forgiven.
be humble.
be purified.
be clean and made ready.
be submitted and obedient.
be all about the Lord.

A praying worshiper knows how Jesus prayed and follows His lead. In John 17, Jesus prayed three different prayers. First, He prayed for Himself, then His disciples, then He finished His prayer by praying for all believers.

First, He prayed for Himself in John 17:1-5.

Jesus spoke these words, lifted up His eyes to heaven, and said, "Father, the hour has come. Glorify Your Son, that Your Son also may glorify You, as You have given Him authority over all flesh, that He should give eternal life to as many as You have given Him. And this is eternal life, that they may know You, the only true God, and Jesus Christ whom You have sent. I have glorified You on the earth. I have finished the work which You have given Me to do. And now, O Father, glorify Me together with Yourself, with the glory which I had with You before the world was."

Then He prayed for His disciples in verses 6-19.

"I have manifested Your name to the men whom You have given Me out of the world. They were Yours, You gave them to Me, and they have kept Your word. Now they have known that all things which You have given Me are from You. For I have given to them the words which You have given Me; and they have received them, and have known surely that I came forth from You; and they have believed that You sent

Me. I pray for them. I do not pray for the world but for those whom You have given Me, for they are Yours. And all Mine are Yours, and Yours are Mine, and I am glorified in them. Now I am no longer in the world, but these are in the world, and I come to You. Holy Father, keep through Your name those whom You have given Me, that they may be one as We are. While I was with them in the world, I kept them in Your name. Those whom You gave Me I have kept; and none of them is lost except the son of perdition, that the Scripture might be fulfilled. But now I come to You, and these things I speak in the world, that they may have My joy fulfilled in themselves. I have given them Your word; and the world has hated them because they are not of the world, just as I am not of the world. I do not pray that You should take them out of the world, but that You should keep them from the evil one. They are not of the world, just as I am not of the world. Sanctify them by Your truth. Your word is truth. As You sent Me into the world, I also have sent them into the world. And for their sakes I sanctify Myself, that they also may be sanctified by the truth."

In verses 20–26, He prayed for all believers.

I do not pray for these alone, but also for those who will believe in Me through their word; that they all may be one, as You, Father, are in Me, and I in You; that they also may be one in Us, that the world may believe that You sent Me. And the glory which You gave Me, I have given them, that they may be one just as We are one; I in them, and You in Me; that they may be made perfect in one, and that the world may know that You have sent Me, and have loved them as You have loved Me. Father, I declare that they also whom You gave Me may be with Me where I am, that they may behold My glory which You have given Me; for You loved Me before the foundations of the world. O righteous Father! The world has not known You, but I have known

You; and these have known that You sent Me. And I have declared to them Your name, and will declare it, that the love with which You loved Me may be in them, and I in them."

This same time in Jesus' prayer life has been recorded in the book of Luke in chapter 22:39-46.

Coming out, He went to the Mount of Olives, as He was accustomed, and His disciples also followed Him. When He came to the place, He said to them, "Pray that you may not enter into temptation." And He was withdrawn from them about a stone's throw, and He knelt down and prayed, saying, "Father, if it is Your will, take this cup away from Me; nevertheless not My will, but Yours, be done." Then an angel appeared to Him from heaven, strengthening Him. And being in agony, He prayed more earnestly. Then His sweat became like great drops of blood falling down to the ground. When He rose up from prayer, and had come to His disciples, He found them sleeping from sorrow. Then He said to them, "Why do you sleep? Rise and pray, lest you enter into temptation."

Sometimes intercessory prayer can be agonizing as it was for Jesus. Even the act of submission can cost us so much, as it did Jesus, that our physical bodies can have a negative response. Jesus was in such pain and distress that His blood vessels began to break as a result of the heavy load and stress of what was about to take place. He went to His Father God to ask if there was another way to accomplish the same result, but apparently the Father God did not change the plan. Then Jesus submitted His earthly and divine will to the will of the Father for all mankind, but not without a cost in His prayer life. He became so stressed that the blood vessels popped and His sweat was filled with His own blood. That moment, in a sense, was Jesus' first place to shed His blood for us - in His own will to surrender to the plan of God. Submission caused Him to shed His sinless blood. It was the beginning of total submission.

When we pray, if it is not the beginning of total submission for us, then we should not approach the throne of God! Submission, humility, accountability, purity, and integrity are the characteristics the Father is looking for in the high seat of a worshiper. If you cannot give up your way and take on His way, then move over, and allow someone else in that place at His feet. The Lord will raise up worshipers who will truly worship Him!

God's kind of worshiper is an intercessor. A true worshiper can lay his own life aside to stand in the gap for the entire group. God is looking for, searching the entire earth's surface for those who are willing, yes, willing to lay down everything for the cause of Christ. Is this person who you truly are? If not, yet, is it who you long to be? That's what it takes… a longing to be who you are called and created to be! God will do the rest. Give yourself to Him, and He will cause your thoughts to become agreeable to His will.

Proverbs 16:3
Roll your works upon the Lord [commit and trust them wholly to Him; He will cause your thoughts to become agreeable to His will, and] so shall your plans be established and succeed. (Amplified Bible)

A groaning prayer. A moaning prayer. A sighing prayer.

Jesus said in John 12:26-32, *"If anyone serves Me, let him follow Me; and where I am, there My servant will be also. If anyone serves Me, him My Father will honor. Now My soul is troubled, and what shall I say? 'Father, save Me from this hour'? But for this purpose I came to this hour. Father, glorify Your name." Then a voice came from heaven, saying, "I have both glorified it and will glorify it again." Therefore the people who stood by and heard it said that it had thundered. Others said, "An angel has spoken to Him." Jesus answered and said, "This voice did not come because of Me, but for your sake. Now is the judgment of this world; now the ruler of this world will be cast out. And I, if I am lifted up from the earth, will draw all peoples to Myself."*

We must be careful to have our ears tuned to the sounds of the Spirit of God. For in this passage some heard the sounds from heaven as mere thunder while others said that angels were speaking! We need to learn to be able to discern what is supernatural and what is natural and this can only be done through prayer, real prayer. The rote repetition of words, or even the ritual speaking of God's biblical words over and over, is not what true prayer is. God's kind of prayer is touching heaven, and allowing heaven to touch us. Jesus taught us how to pray when He said to the disciples in Matthew 6:9-13, Our *Father in heaven, hallowed be Your name. Your kingdom come. Your will be done on earth as it is in heaven. Give us this day our daily bread. And forgive us our debts, as we forgive our debtors. And do not lead us into temptation, but deliver us from the evil one. For Yours is the kingdom and the power and the glory forever. Amen.*

Jesus was teaching the disciples and ultimately we who worship that prayer is about relationship. By calling God, "Our Father," we are personalizing our connection with God, as our own personal Father. Jesus could have said, "My Father," but He did not. He was teaching us, and including us in this divine relationship.

Then Jesus taught us that reverence and holiness is the ultimate understanding of divine relationship with the

Father. The Father is holy, divine, to be hallowed, and respected! *The fear of the Lord is the beginning of wisdom.* (Psalm 111:10)

Calling God's kingdom forth in our prayer life is a powerful part of submission to His ultimate will and purpose for our lives. "Lord, we call forth Your kingdom to this earth." It is acknowledging that His kingdom exists in heaven, but we long for it to exist in our personal lives and in our worship. We call forth the kingdom of heaven to the earth! "Kingdom of God, come forth!" God's will is complete in heaven, and God's will is complete in my earthly life also. I pray this and agree with it.

By these words in prayer we are submitting our lives to His kingdom will; no longer do we live for what we can personally gain on this earth, but we submit our lives, the sum of it, and all its parts to kingdom business, and ultimately to the will of God. This brings about a "giving of oneself" to Him fully and completely. This is what the Father God has asked for from us. He wants all of us so He can give us all of Him!

Once we have submitted ourselves completely to Him, then we can accept and fully expect for Him to, *Give us this day, our daily bread; and forgive us our debts, as we forgive our debtors.* We want all of His portion, so we must be willing to empty ourselves of our earthly portion. His portion has eternal and everlasting power, our earthly portion does not.

Then the ultimate of admissions comes when we further lift Him up saying, *For Yours is the kingdom, the power, and the glory forever!* In our vernacular, "This is all about You, and not about me, forever!" This takes our eyes off ourselves and finishes it with the amen of all amens, forever!

There are times when praying cannot be put into the words of our society for whatever reasons. There are prayers that cannot be uttered; some that cost so much of ourselves that only groans, moans, and sighs become audible. This is when the Spirit of God can pray through us, bringing about the realm of heaven all around us that cannot be reached through our conscience mind any longer. These places are too deep, or too high, or both, for our mere human abilities.

In Romans 8:26-28, *Meanwhile, the moment we get tired in the waiting, God's Spirit is right alongside helping us along. If we don't know how or what to pray, it doesn't matter. He does our praying in and for us, making prayer out of our wordless sighs, our aching groans. He knows us far better than we know ourselves, knows our pregnant condition, and keeps us present before God. That's why we can be so sure that every detail in our lives of love for God is worked into something good. (Message Bible)*

"Wordless sighs" and *"aching groans"* are two phrases that true intercessors are very familiar with in prayer. This is a level in our prayer lives when we give up any rational and logical language and opt for a language of angels that is spoken by the Holy Spirit praying through us.

Luke 11:10-13 states, *For everyone who asks receives, and he who seeks finds, and to him who knocks it will be opened. If a son asks for bread from any father among you, will he give him a stone? Or if he asks for a fish, will he give him a serpent instead of a fish? Or if he asks for an egg, will he offer him a scorpion? If you then, being evil, know how to give good gifts to your children, how much more will your heavenly Father give the Holy Spirit to those who ask Him!*

If you are not filled with the Holy Spirit, it is a simple matter of asking the Father who promises that He will give to you, just because you ask!

Acts 2:4
And they were all filled with the Holy Spirit and began to speak with other tongues, as the Spirit gave them utterance.

This is not complicated. God is who He says that He is. The Holy Spirit is who God says. God says any and all can be filled with the Holy Spirit and can utilize the gift of the Spirit of God through praying in another tongue, another language, a language that bypasses the natural understanding of the brain, thereby giving access to the Holy Spirit to pray through us at a higher and more powerful level than human understanding.

Lord, I give myself to You, completely.

We have already read Romans 8:26-28 and we understand how the Spirit of God longs to pray through us. The power of being spirit-filled is the ability to utilize any and all areas of who we are for the kingdom of God. The power of our intercessory prayer life in worship is the use of all levels of who we are by the Spirit of God. I Corinthians 14:15 states, *What is the conclusion then? I will pray with the spirit, and I will also pray with the understanding. I will sing with the spirit, and I will also sing with the understanding.*

There are times when our human mind cannot comprehend what is necessary in prayer or even in worship. There are other times when we need to stay in the language of the people in the room for their edification and understanding. The Lord knows all; He knows and will direct through His Spirit. He is the ultimate orchestration, and conductor for the symphony of prayer that should be coming through us at all times as we live and breathe and have our being!

II Corinthians 5:2-4, *For in this we groan, earnestly desiring to be clothed with our habitation which is from heaven, if indeed, having been clothed, we shall not be found naked. For we who are in this tent groan, being burdened, not because we want to be unclothed, but further clothed, that mortality may be swallowed up by life.*

Once the Spirit of God has taken root within us, even our flesh groans to be more like Him and less like ourselves. These are sounds from the earth realm that no human words can express, but God hears our cries. These sound waves of the human soul which cannot be uttered with mankind's understanding come up to the feet of Jesus with sweet smells and fragrances of worship far beyond any human ability to pray or worship!

Psalm 130:1-2
Out of the depths I have cried to You, O Lord; Lord, hear my voice! Let Your ears be attentive to the voice of my supplications.

Psalm 22:5
They cried to You, and were delivered; They trusted in You, and were not ashamed.

"Lord, listen to our cries. Hear those sounds within us that are too deep, too broken to be spoken with human words or even sounds. Hear our hearts in intercession and worship before Your throne, day and night, we cry out!"

Jesus told His disciples to pray to stay out of temptation. Since the greatest problem with worshipers for several generations has been sin, obviously there has not been enough prayer to keep worshipers away from temptation. We cannot assume that just because we are close to the Lord, or because we have the giftings and talents that allow us to come to Him that others will follow. We cannot assume that this causes us to be exempt from sin. In fact, it is the opposite. No one in Jesus' days upon the earth was in closer proximity to God in flesh than the disciples, but Jesus warned them to pray, pray, pray to resist temptation.

We can't do away with temptation. The devil and his demons are on the earth for a period of time in which we have no control over the end. So we must follow the instructions we have been given to keep our lives clean and pure before the throne of God. Jesus gave simple and specific instructions. Pray! Pray! Pray!

If you want to stand in the office of worshiper, then you must stay clean and pure before Him. You must stay separated and holy unto God. If we want to stay in right-standing with God, we must follow this one simple instruction from Jesus to His disciples to pray! There are no substitutes or time lines. We never can be good enough to not have to pray. We can never get so good at what we do to not have to pray. Our talents, giftings, callings, positioning or any such thing can't take us to the place where we can resist temptation. We need prayer and lots of it.

So you want to be a worshiper; you want to stand on the platform and sing or play an instrument, or dance before the Lord, or be on the drama team? Then first, and I mean first, you must learn to pray, and most importantly, you must learn how to stay consistent in prayer. When you make prayer and intimacy with the King of kings your one goal, your life pursuit, then maybe, just maybe you can stay clean enough to serve God in worship.

Worship is a high calling, one with many temptations, and pitfalls. We must learn how to be aware of each and every one without falling snare to any of them. We must learn to be wise, truly wise, without pride, or an elevated mind. Humility is the beginning of all things and all positions in the kingdom of God. Humility in our lives is birthed upon our knees, ever pushing out 'self,' pride, and a need to be noticed and approved. As we push these self-promoting aspects of human nature out of our being, then humility can fill the void within us and a worshiper can be born.

If you still want to be seen, then you are not there yet. If you still want to be heard, then you are not there yet. If you need to be the one who sings the solo, or plays the instrumental break, or has to stand in the front, then you are not there yet. If your mind is upon anything or anyone other than Jesus Christ and Him glorified, then you are not there yet. Pray, pray, pray without ceasing. Why? Because when we finally arrive with all of our "self" nailed to the cross, then after a little bit of time, and I mean, minutes, flesh begins to take over once again. We are ever in constant warfare against our own flesh, keeping it under so Jesus Christ can be lifted high.

The rote repetition of words is not *what* true prayer *is.* God's kind of prayer *is* touching heaven, *and allowing* heaven *to* touch us.

Chapter Six Questions:

1. What do I have in my life when my mind is fixed on anything other than who He is?
______________________ and ______________________.

2. What are worshipers created to do?

____

____

____

3. What is God searching the earth looking for?

____

____

____

4. What must be found in our worship of the Father?

____

____

____

5. What should the presence of God make us want to do?

____

____

____

6. Do I meet the prerequisites of a worshiper?

____

____

____

7. According to John 17, how did Jesus pray?

____

____

____

____

8. Am I willing to completely submit myself to my heavenly Father, knowing there is a price that comes with submission?

____

____

____

9. What kind of worshiper is "God's kind of worshiper?"

____

____

____

10. True discernment of the natural vs. the supernatural comes only through much ____________________.

11. I am taught to pray in what passage of scripture?

____

____

____

12. Why does God want all of me?

____

____

____

13. What is the power of being spirit-filled?

____

____

____

14. What is the first thing I must learn to do (and be consistent in doing) in order to be a worshiper?

____

____

____

Chapter Seven
A Humble Worshiper

Psalm 9:11-12
Sing praises to the Lord, who dwells in Zion! Declare His deeds among the people. When He avenges blood, He remembers them; He does not forget the cry of the humble.

Psalm 10:17
Lord, You have heard the desire of the humble; You will prepare their heart; You will cause Your ear to hear.

All pride must go. We must learn to humble ourselves in worship before Him. It is not about us, you or me! This is about Him, His presence, His purpose and His will!

Jesus gives us through His Word a wonderful example of what is true and pure and humble in the following chapter in the book of Mark. As we read together, notice how the Lord longs to help us change. His desire is for us is to be different, to be acceptable, and He is willing to give us the time we need to change. But if we do not make the adjustments needed, then He will do what He will do.

Mark 11:1-11
Now when they drew near Jerusalem, to Bethphage and Bethany, at the Mount of Olives, He sent two of His disciples; and He said to them, "Go into the village opposite you; and as soon as you have entered it you will find a colt tied, on which no one has sat. Loose it and bring it. And if anyone says to you, 'Why are you doing this?' say, 'The Lord has need of it,' and immediately he will send it here."

So they went their way, and found the colt tied by the door outside on the street, and they loosed it. But some of those who stood there said to them, "What are you doing, loosing the colt?" And they spoke to them just as Jesus had commanded. So they let them go. Then they brought the colt to Jesus and threw their clothes on it, and He sat on it. And many spread their clothes on the road, and others cut down leafy branches from the trees and spread them on the road. Then those who went before and those who followed cried out, saying:

"Hosanna! Blessed is He who comes in the name of the Lord!" Blessed is the kingdom of our father David that comes in the name of the Lord! Hosanna in the highest!"

And Jesus went into Jerusalem and into the temple. So when He had looked around at all things, as the hour was already late, He went out to Bethany with the twelve.

The people gathered together and laid their clothes and palm branches from the trees on the ground giving entrance to Jesus to ride into Jerusalem as honored and lifted up with all authority. Jesus came in riding a donkey which had never been ridden before, as the people cried out in worship, "Hosanna!" These cries of worship ultimately gave Jesus permission to come in to their hearts and lives and take a look around as is illustrated in verses 9-11.

Picking up the story again… as Jesus came into Jerusalem, He went to the temple and went inside. But Jesus was not a priest in the eyes of the people and according to the religious folks. He was not from the tribe of Levi, but was from the tribe of Judah. He was only given access to the outer courts of the temple. The inner courts and holy of holies was only accessed by the priests from the tribe of Levi.

What was in the outer courts? There were tables set up with those buying and selling sacrifices and Jesus came in and looked around. The Bible says that Jesus went in and "looked around." What was there that was so disturbing to Jesus that He took the time to walk around and look at it all? Jesus was walking in His authority that had been given Him by those who worshiped Him as He entered Jerusalem. Was He upset that they were selling sacrifices? Probably not, since it had been set up in the Old Testament and under the law that if it was too difficult to bring your sacrifice or offering from a great distance to sell it where you lived, and then buy what you needed once you arrived at the temple. So it was not the selling of the sacrifices that was disturbing Him. What was upsetting to Jesus was the fact that the money changers were making money hand over fist, working with the crooked priests. It was not that they were prospering, but that they were crooked in their business.

It was their hearts, their methods, their crooked and perverse ways of dealing, of doing business, that had His undivided attention. You see, the practice of that time was that the temple priests and the merchants in the outer courts had gone into business together. What were they doing? They were cheating the people. There were priests who stood in the outer courts to examine the animals that people had brought for sacrifice. Those animals could not have any defects at all. They had to have straight horns, no blind eyes, and needed to be as perfect as possible for giving to the Lord in sacrifice.

The priests and the merchants had made a money-making deal for themselves. The priests would not accept the sacrifice the people had brought with them, even if it was perfectly acceptable. They would reject it and by rejecting it, the people were forced to have to purchase another animal from the merchants in the outer courts. The priests would then take the rejected animal and circle around back and put the so-called rejected animal in the pen with all the other animals for selling later on to another unsuspecting person. Then when someone else came along with their sacrifice, the dirty-dealing priests would reject that animal too, confiscate it, and thereby sell the previously rejected animal to the next person coming to sacrifice to the Lord. The merchants and priests would share in the profits as they lied to the people. What a racket they had going!

Jesus knew what they were doing and as He came in to the temple, into the outer courts and had a look around. I can imagine Him strolling through this area, stopping at each merchant's table, examining their operation. I can just see His gaze level in on the merchant behind the table, giving him the "once over." Jesus must have stared intently into those sin-filled eyes… a chance to repent perhaps? Can you hear the sound of the Spirit of God speaking to the merchant through the "look" coming from Jesus? The unspoken words must have been something like, "I see you. I know what you are doing. I know your crooked and perverse heart. I am giving you time to change and repent. You don't have a long time."

With that piercing and convicting look, Jesus would have turned and walked to the next table to examine that person's stack of money, his crooked and lying ways, and give him the "Jesus look." From table to table, Jesus walked around and examined the dealings of those buying and selling, stealing and cheating the people. It was only a matter of time. Their days were numbered down to one day. Jesus had given them 24 hours to get it right with the Father God. But as He walked away, no one changed; everyone stayed the same. Not one of them repented, so He came back the following day after they had been given plenty of time to make amends and stop their lying and cheating. A day later, Jesus returned, after giving ample time for them to repent and change their habits, but no one had repented. Money still ruled their hearts.

The Bible says that Jesus overturned their tables. He disrupted their cheating game and caused their ugly, sinful schemes to be exposed to one and all. The merchants became fearful and began to plot and plan to destroy Him… why? Why then?

Isn't this how sin works? When sin becomes exposed or we are afraid it is about to be exposed, we become angry, fearful, full of blame, trying to hide our sinful ways! But there is no hiding from God. Pride is such an ugly sin!

Jesus' life was safe as long as He healed the poor and blind, but once He started messing with their income, all hell was about to be unleashed on the King of kings, the Messiah, the Lamb of God! Can you imagine how they must have conspired together? He must be stopped. They would destroy the One who would dare question their hearts and their actions! He would have to be done away with; He would have to be removed. He could not stay. He could not remain among the people. Before He got in their business He was relatively harmless, but after He stepped in, examining their sacrificial business practices and took authority that was rightfully His, abolishing the crooked and perverse money changers, He had to be removed from among the people. The best way would be cunning and conniving, dirty-dealing of course, but what else was new? That had been their way for so long they didn't even recognize their sin any more. It had taken root, and had after a long time, taken their hearts as well.

Mark 11:12-19

Now the next day, when they had come out from Bethany, He was hungry. And seeing from afar a fig tree having leaves, He went to see if perhaps He would find something on it.

When He came to it, He found nothing but leaves, for it was not the season for figs. In response Jesus said to it, "Let no one eat fruit from you ever again." And His disciples heard it.

So they came to Jerusalem. Then Jesus went into the temple and began to drive out those who bought and sold in the temple, and overturned the tables of the money changers and the seats of those who sold doves. And He would not allow anyone to carry wares through the temple. Then He taught, saying to them, "Is it not written, 'My house shall be called a house of prayer for all nations'? But you have made it a 'den of thieves.'"

And the scribes and chief priests heard it and sought how they might destroy Him; for they feared Him, because all the people were astonished at His teaching. When evening had come, He went out of the city.

Some folks like to describe the passage above as if Jesus threw a holy fit. But this was not the case. Jesus had walked in with His God-given authority, and had given them opportunity to stop what they were doing, but no one had stopped. So He came back 24 hours later to "clean house" for His Father. He came in and turned the tables over, not in a fit of rage, but in all authority, and He spoke the truth to them.

When we worship Him as they did, as He rode into Jerusalem, we give Him the right to come into our lives, walk around, look around, and show us what it is we need to change. He comes in like the ultimate interior decorator of life, and points out those things that need to be changed within us. He longs to help us be different, be holy, be righteous, and be pure before Him. He longs to come in and not have to turn the tables over in our lives, but to simply tell us where and what needs to be done differently. Then He gives us time to change these things ourselves. When He returns and looks around again, if He sees those recommendations put into practice in our hearts, minds, and lives, then He is pleased and our worship is acceptable. But if after He has given to us those things we need to move around, move out of us, rearrange, etc. and we do nothing about it, then when He comes back and takes another look around, He could be doing some table overturning in our lives!

I would rather take the time to rearrange by repentance those things in my life that need to be changed. I don't want the Lord to have to come back in and have to do the redecorating and renovating process Himself by overturning things in my life! Jesus always gives us ample opportunity to humble ourselves before Him and repent.

Repent - "to burn the house to the ground."

"Repent" means to "burn the house to the ground" in ancient Hebrew. It is the word-picture from a story that goes like this. In ancient times, armies would march in and take over an entire city, taking the people hostage. As they were leaving the city, once they got a safe distance away, the hostages were told to look back at their homes, while the armies would burn them to the ground! As they watched, this was supposed to solidify within them the fact that there was nowhere for them to return. Their homes were gone; their city was destroyed thus causing them to never want to go back again. They had no more pasts to long for.

In our lives, the Lord wants us to burn our pasts to the ground, leaving nothing behind for us to long to return to along the way. Repentance is not punishment, but it is separation from the old ways of thinking, and being. Repentance is a heart and mind change, a repositioning of ones' soul so that the past is as if it never existed!

God's kind of humility leaves no room for looking back and longing to return to the old person, or past way of life. God's kind of humility is with bended knee, ever before the throne in worship to the One true King of kings! Humility is like a cloak we must wear to be presentable in the presence of Almighty God. To take a statement from a vision received by Rick Joyner and written in the book, *The Final Quest,* concerning humility, this was a conversation between Rick in his vision and the persona of Wisdom.

This section is entitled, **"The Power of Pride."** It reads,

"I was pondering how I was learning as much by descending the mountain as I had by climbing it when the noise from the battlefield drew my attention. By now there were thousands of the mighty warriors who had crossed the plain to attack the remnant of the enemy horde. The enemy was fleeing in all directions, except for the one division, Pride. Completely undetected, it had marched right up to the rear of the advancing warriors, and was about to release a hail of arrows. It was then that I noticed the mighty warriors had no armor on their backsides. They were totally exposed and vulnerable to what was about to hit them.

Wisdom then remarked, *"You have taught that there was no armor for the backside, which meant that you were vulnerable if you ran from the enemy. However, you never saw how advancing in pride also made you vulnerable."*

I could only nod in acknowledgement. It was too late to do anything, and it was almost unbearable to watch, but Wisdom said that I must. I knew that the kingdom of God was about to suffer a major defeat. I had felt sorrow before, but I had never felt this kind of sorrow.

To my amazement, when the arrows of pride struck the warriors they did not even notice. However, the enemy kept shooting. The warriors were bleeding and getting weaker fast, but they would not acknowledge it. Soon they were too weak to hold up their shields and swords; they cast them down, declaring that they no longer needed them. They started taking off their armor, saying it was not needed anymore either.

Then another enemy division appeared and moved up swiftly. It was called Strong Delusion. Its members released a hail of arrows and they all seemed to hit their mark. Just a few of the demons of delusion, who were all small and seemingly weak, led away this once great army of glorious warriors. They were taken to different prison camps, each named after a different doctrine of demons. I was astounded at how this great company of the righteous had been so easily defeated, and they still did not even know what had hit them.

I blurted out, "How could those who were so strong, who have been all the way to the top of the mountain, who have seen the Lord as they have, be so vulnerable?"

"Pride is the hardest enemy to see, and it always sneaks up behind you,"* Wisdom lamented. *"In some ways, those who have been to the greatest heights are in the greatest danger of falling. You must always remember that in this life you can fall at any time from any level."

"Take heed when you think you stand, lest you fall," I replied. "How awesome these Scriptures seem to me now."

***"When you think you are the least vulnerable to falling is in fact when you are the most vulnerable. Most men fall immediately after a great victory,"* Wisdom lamented.**

"How can we keep from being attacked like this?" I asked.

"Stay close to me, inquire of the Lord before making major decisions, and keep that mantle on. Then the enemy will not be able to easily blind side you as he did those."

I looked at my mantle. It looked so plain and insignificant. I felt that it made me look more like a homeless person than a warrior. Wisdom responded as if I had been speaking out loud.

"The Lord is closer to the homeless than to kings. You only have true strength to the degree that you walk in the grace of God, and He gives His grace to the humble. No evil weapon can penetrate this mantle, because nothing can overpower His grace. As long as you wear this mantle you are safe from this kind of attack."

I then started to look up to see how many warriors were still on the mountain. I was shocked to see how few there were. I noticed, however, that they all had on the same mantle of humility. "How did that happen?" I inquired.

***"When they saw the battle you just witnessed, they all came to me for help, and I gave them their mantles,"* Wisdom replied.**

"But I thought you were with me that whole time?"

***"I am with all who go forth to do the will of My Father,"* Wisdom answered.**

"You're the Lord!" I cried.

"Yes,"* He answered. *"I told you that I would never leave you or forsake you. I am with all of My warriors just as I am with you. I will be to you whatever you need to

accomplish My will, and you have needed wisdom.” **Then He vanished.**

There was so much more to gain from this book in the next section that I felt we should read on a little further. The next section is called, **“Rank in the Kingdom.”** Read on…

I was left standing in the midst of the great company of angels who were ministering to the wounded on the level of “Salvation.” As I began to walk past these angels, they bowed to one knee and showed me great respect. I finally asked one of them why they did this, as even the smallest was much more powerful than I was. “Because of the mantle,” he replied. “That is the highest rank in the kingdom.”

“This is just a plain mantle,” I protested.

“No!” the angel protested. “You are clothed in the grace of God. There is no greater power than that!”

“But there are thousands of us all wearing the same mantle. How could it represent rank?” I asked.

“You are the dreaded champions, the sons and daughters of the King. He wore the same mantle when He walked on this earth. As long as you are clothed in that, there is no power in heaven or earth that can stand before you. Everyone in heaven and hell recognizes that mantle. We are indeed His servants, but He abides in you, and you are clothed in His grace.”

Somehow I knew that if I had not been wearing the mantle, and if my glorious armor had been exposed, that the angel’s statement, and their behavior toward me, would have fed my pride. It was simply impossible to feel prideful or arrogant while wearing such a drab, plain

cloak. However, my confidence in the mantle was growing fast."

Can you see in this passage taken from Rick Joyner's vision that what looks plain, even drab and ugly to us when wearing humility, looks like authority to those who are watching us? The Bible makes these statements plainly to us, but the portion of this vision paints an undeniable picture of the power of humility versus the destruction of pride. We must not approach the throne of God in prideful worship for it will bring about such destruction that we cannot bear it. We must approach the throne of God in a humble and contrite condition, understanding our position and who is who in the realm of worship.

Psalm 147:6
The Lord lifts up the humble; He casts the wicked down to the ground.

In this particular passage of scripture the "wicked" people are the prideful people. The amazing part to me is that this humility verse is followed immediately with a verse about worship.

Psalm 147:7
Sing to the Lord with thanksgiving; Sing praises on the harp to our God.

Humility is an open door for the Lord to come forth and sit upon our worship and praise, to be lifted up in adoration as King of kings and Lord of lords.

James 4:6-10
But He gives more grace. Therefore He says: "God resists the proud, but gives grace to the humble." Therefore submit to God. Resist the devil and he will flee from you. Draw near

to God and He will draw near to you. Cleanse your hands, you sinners; and purify your hearts, you double-minded. Lament and mourn and weep! Let your laughter be turned to mourning and your joy to gloom. Humble yourselves in the sight of the Lord, and He will lift you up.

Matthew 18:4
Therefore whoever humbles himself as this little child is the greatest in the kingdom of heaven.

The Word Wealth section at this verse in the *Spirit-Filled Life Bible* gives us the Greek word for "humble." It is the word "tapeinoo," which is pronounced as ('tap-eye-nah-oh'). In the *Strong's Concordance* it is referenced as #5013 with the literal definition "to make low." It is used in reference to a mountain in Luke 3:5. Metaphorically, the word means "to debase, humble, lower oneself." It describes "a person who is devoid of all arrogance and self-exaltation - a person who is willingly submitted to God and His will."

If we can simply apply this basic definition of humility to our own personal lives in worship we can see how we can rightfully take our position at His feet. But there is no other entrance without humility.

All pride must go. We must learn to *humble* ourselves in *worship* before Him.
It is not about us, you or me!
This is about Him -
His presence, His purpose and *His will!*

Chapter Seven Questions:

1. What did the cries of worship allow to happen in the lives of the people in the Mark 11 passage?

____

____

____

____

2. What did Jesus observe in the temple (in the merchants) that made Him so upset?

____

____

____

____

3. Why did Jesus leave the temple and come back the next day?

____

____

____

____

4. Pure, honest worship gives Jesus entrance into our hearts and lives so He can do what?

____

____

____

____

5. What must we do after He has examined our hearts and lives?

____

____

____

____

6. According to the passage from Rick Joyner's book, what is the hardest enemy to see?

____

____

____

____

7. According to the passage from Rick Joyner's book, who are we to stay close to?

____

____

____

____

8. According to the passage from Rick Joyner's book, who does God give grace to?

____

____

____

____

9. According to the passage from Rick Joyner's book, who is Wisdom? ____________________

10. According to the passage from Rick Joyner's book, there is no greater power than to be clothed in ______________.

11. Approaching the throne of God in prideful worship can only bring ____________________.

12. How must we approach the throne of God?
In what manner or condition?

____

____

____

____

Chapter Eight
A Pure Worshiper

Proverbs 16:2
All the ways of a man are pure in his own eyes, but the Lord weighs the spirits.

Proverbs 15:26
The thoughts of the wicked are an abomination to the Lord, but the words of the pure are pleasant.

Proverbs 20:9
Who can say, "I have made my heart clean, I am pure from my sin?"

Job 15:14-16
What is man, that he could be pure? And he who is born of a woman, that he could be righteous? If God puts no trust in His saints, and the heavens are not pure in His sight, how much less man, who is abominable and filthy, who drinks iniquity like water!

Job 25:5
If even the moon does not shine, and the stars are not pure in His sight...

Psalm 12:6
The words of the Lord are pure words, like silver tried in a furnace of earth, purified seven times....

Psalm 18:26
With the pure You will show Yourself pure...

Psalm 73:1-2
Truly God is good to Israel, to such as are pure in heart. But

as for me, my feet had almost stumbled; My steps had nearly slipped.

A plea for purity is being sent forth from the very presence of God!

I Thessalonians 4:1-8
Finally then, brethren, we urge and exhort in the Lord Jesus that you should abound more and more, just as you received from us how you ought to walk and to please God; for you know what commandments we gave you through the Lord Jesus. For this is the will of God, your sanctification: that you should abstain from sexual immorality; that each of you should know how to possess his own vessel in sanctification and honor, not in passion of lust, like the Gentiles who do not know God; that no one should take advantage of and defraud his brother in this matter, because the Lord is the avenger of all such, as we also forewarned you and testified. For God did not call us to uncleanness, but in holiness. Therefore he who rejects this does not reject man, but God, who has also given us His Holy Spirit.

Our God has a definite plan of purity for those who say they are called to Him. His will is specified as sanctification in this above passage of scripture. What is "sanctification"? Quite simply, it means "set apart as unto the Lord." When we are set apart from the impure, then we must represent the Lord in all things, all parts of our lives, from our daily choices, our tongues, our actions, who we hang with, in everything. There are no gray areas or blurred lines in purity. Either we are or we are not. It is not about works, or laws, or rules. Sanctification is based upon our hearts towards God, how much of ourselves are we willing to give Him, and how much of our flesh are we willing to allow the Spirit of God to consume. The real test comes in realizing that we cannot have it both ways. We cannot be mostly pure with a few smaller undisclosed areas left to wallow in the mud. No, with God, it is all or nothing. He either wants all of us, or He wants none of us. Purity is a choice made to trust God in everything and with everything.

Purity is not in our abilities, power, or authority. God's kind of purity is solely based upon the heart, and no man can know another person's heart. But God knows; He knows everything. Nothing is hidden from Him. He longs to purify us with His gaze, for us to dive into the depths of those amazingly purifying eyes of His, head first, saying as we go under for the third time, "I am Yours."

When our hearts are toward purity, then our actions will follow. We will choose to live clean, and separate ourselves from those who are not pure. Our hearts will guide us to close the door on those things, and people who tend to lead us away from the fire of God. When our hearts are running after God's heart we will no longer have time to long for the things of this earth.

Purity in this earth realm cannot be earned. It is impossible for humans to create within themselves any sense of true purity. That is why the ultimate sacrifice of the pure and sinless Lamb of God had to be presented to take away the sins of the world. There was no human who could do this. Mankind did their best at this for thousands of years only to fail miserably. The sacrifice of God's only Son, Jesus, was the only way.

Purity is never achieved, only accepted. It does not come like fairy dust upon us, but comes out of the testing and intense heat of God's kind of fire. It comes with the pouring out of the top portion of the wine, leaving the dregs of impurity at the bottom. It does not come without the price of giving of one's self, of being poured out over and over again until finally, purity is attained. With each pouring period of time, it will always be followed by a time of waiting, of the dregs of impurity to settle down to the bottom of our "vessel" so we can be poured out again, and again. It is a long and painful process; in fact, this time frame covers exactly the time span called life. It takes a lifetime to achieve this level of purity. Well, as I said before, it is not really an achievement, for we can claim no accolades or rewards for it. We are simply the yielded vessel being poured out repeatedly. It is a lifetime process. Once deemed ready by the "pourer," we are allowed to leave this place and stand amazed in His presence. Whether there in the physical or mental realm or by the spirit, I do not know; I only know that once we are prepared and made ready then we can come into His presence.

Purity is about being holy. Holiness is the evidence of a pure heart. It is about longevity. Holiness and purity are not about our pasts, or what we have gone through. It is about our choice today and every day after this one. Purity is a way of life, a choice made that is with us for eternity. Purity is not an option or even a good idea with our Lord. It is a must. Psalm 29:2 states, *Give unto the Lord the glory due to His name; Worship the Lord in the beauty of holiness.*

Holy and pure are synonyms. Purity and holiness are prerequisites of entering in to the Holy of Holies. We must be purified and made holy by His blood, before we can enter into His presence. Holiness is beautiful before the King. When we approach Him with our hearts and lives made clean and ready before Him, He sees us as beautiful!

Purity and holiness… prerequisites of entering the Holy of Holies.

We have, for far too long, moved the lines of accountability and integrity, purity and holiness, until for the casual observer, it is hard to distinguish between what is godly and what is not godly. No matter how well a human being has learned to mask or hide behind the camouflage of much "doing" God knows our hearts. God knows who we really are, or who we are not. There is no use in trying to pretend.

As I said before, purity is not fairy dust dropped upon our heads at the altar; it is not a personality trait that certain people have and others do not. Purity is a choice to live for the Lord with no excuses. There is no justifying those things we hold on to because of "such and such." When we make a choice to be in Him, we must decide how we are going to live, forever. There is nothing from our pasts that is good enough to use as an excuse for our present choices.

Are we going to mess up? Are we going to fail and even fall at times? Of course, we will. All of us have sinned and at some point we all make wrong choices. It is not possible to live holy and pure without realizing that we simply cannot do it on our own. It is impossible for us to be holy or to be pure without completely losing ourselves within the person of Jesus Christ. Purity is not a destiny any human being is capable of reaching or becoming. We can only accept this precious position in the presence and power of Jesus Christ ever present in our lives and hearts.

The fires of adversity will come in life. They are inevitable. This may not be a popular statement but it is the truth. Jesus told us through His own words in John 16 that in this world we will have troubles, trials, frustrations and distresses. But He made it clear that even though these things would come, not to worry. Jesus had already overcome them all, and had deprived them of any power to harm us. That's a powerful statement! For some of us who have gone through some fairly hard things, if we focus on the statement that "these things have been deprived of power to harm us," we might miss the point here. These things have been eternally deprived of any power to harm our future within Christ! This is the truth. There is not one circumstance or situation that has enough power to change our eternal outcome, apart from our own free will and choice. No matter what happens in my life, good or bad, I still have every right to choose to live for Christ, to live in faith, and if I must, to die in faith. This is my choice. It's yours too.

I choose to live holy, not in my own ability but hidden deep within Christ. I choose to live pure because of the blood of Jesus Christ that cleanses me from all unrighteousness. That makes me clean, pure and righteous through Christ. With all of these things addressed: pure living, holy living and righteous living, we can see that for a worshiper, it is not an "option." We either do it, or we don't. There is no gray area, no riding the fence, no a little in, a little out.

So what will it be for you, God's called and appointed worshiper? Will you live holy and pure before Him? It's possible but you must decide. We will worship in truth and spirit. We will worship by choice. No one can make me worship God. I choose to worship Him by my choice and by my life. Worship is not about a gathering of people. Worship is not about a feeling or a certain section of a service, or even music. Worship is who I am, who I am created to be, eternally. I am becoming worship for the King of kings each and every day of my life… I will worship. When you decide to be His worship also, then *we will worship.*

Chapter Eight Questions:

1. According to I Thessalonians 4:1-8, what is the Lord requiring of His people, (His worshipers)?

____

____

____

____

____

____

2. What can cause us to no longer have time to long for the things of this earth?

____

____

____

____

____

____

3. Where does purity come from? Can it be achieved?

____

____

____

____

____

____

4. What is the evidence of a pure heart?

____

____

____

____

____

____

5. Name two prerequisites for entering the Holy of Holies.

1.

2.

6. What is the only thing that has the power to harm my future with Christ?

____
____
____
____
____
____

7. Will you make the choice to live holy and pure, hidden deep inside of Him? Use this space to journal!

____
____
____
____
____
____
____
____
____
____
____
____
____
____

Chapter Nine
A Worshiper of Integrity

Psalm 26:11-12
But as for me, I will walk in my integrity; redeem me and be merciful to me. My foot stands in an even place; in the congregations I will bless the Lord.

Without integrity we cannot stand in an even place. Without integrity our footing is not solid in the congregation. So how is it that we have so many people who stand on the platform whether in the leaders, or the background singers, or the band, or the choir, who have lost their integrity? How is this possible? Well, I guess it boils down to what I've said before in this book, you might be able to fool some of the people some of the time. But we need to realize that we can never fool God Almighty! He knows our hearts, our pasts, presents, and even our futures.

Integrity is a heart after God's own heart!

Integrity cannot be bought, but must be sought by one whose heart is pure before the Lord. Integrity is not something you can order online from the home shopping network. Integrity is a heart after God's own heart; one who longs more for the will and purposes of God, than for his or her own will and purpose. Integrity is gained over a lifetime but can be lost in a moment.

Ecclesiastes 7:1-4
A good name is better than precious ointment, and the day of death than the day of one's birth; Better to go to the house of mourning than to go to the house of feasting, for that is the end of all men; and the living will take it to heart. Sorrow is better than laughter, for by a sad countenance the heart is made better. The heart of the wise is in the house of mourning but the heart of fools is in the house of mirth.

Your name represents your life, and it gives clarity to your purpose. That's why when we accept Jesus Christ as our Lord and Savior we also accept His name as our own. Much like the bride who says, "I do" and "I will" in the marriage ceremony, she then follows her commitment of words with actions by taking the name of her Bridegroom. We are to do the same with our Bridegroom, Jesus Christ! Once our commitment is made to the Lord for eternity, we are to take His name as our own. Our old life is passed away and we accept the name, and purpose of our eternal Bridegroom, Jesus Christ. His name becomes our name, and we are given the right to use this name and its authority from that point on into eternity. But with this name comes the responsibility of the name's integrity, humility, purity, submission, and purpose. Yes, we get the benefits of this wonderful and magnificent name, but we also must take on the responsibility of this good name, or in our eternal case, God's name through His son, Jesus Christ.

Proverbs 22:1
A good name is to be chosen rather than great riches, loving favor rather than silver and gold.

Isn't it wonderful to know we have the ultimate and highest of all authoritative names in the universe? Jesus Christ is the name we have been given as His own bride. I accept this amazing name and its authority, for I do not earn it, or deserve it. I accept His name as a gift from my beloved to me.

I have heard a lot of people say that we need to "know" the Lord for salvation to be in our lives. I have heard others say we need to "serve" the Lord and that is how we are saved. But the Bible is clear, Jesus Christ must be Lord of our lives! **Lord!** Nothing less than *Lord* qualifies us for salvation and eternal life.

We need to know His name, how to use it, how to cry it out in desperate and deepest broken times. We need to be in such a deep relationship with Him that even before our lips can form the sound of His name that the cry of our heart has already gotten a ready response from the throne of God. But it is so much more than "knowing" His name. Satan knows His name. Demons know His name. Most, if not all, of America knows His name, but that does not mean that when we know His name, we know Him! We must know Him, true! But more importantly does He know you?

Integrity cannot be bought. It must be sought by one whose heart is pure before the Lord.

I know He knows me for I hear Him whisper my name in the night. I know He knows me for I feel His heart when I hurt Him with my insolence and disobedience. I know He knows me for I feel the pull of the deep of Him on my own soul and spirit as I long to know Him more! But how am I certain that He knows my name? I am absolutely certain that He knows my name for He has given me this name! I have taken on His name, as He is my beloved, and I am His!

I am not protecting my name or my reputation anymore. I carry His name; therefore my every choice affects His name! How much more important it is to live for Him and Him alone? How much more important is it to understand the highest honor and responsibility of a true worshiper of the King of kings - to live in righteousness, holiness, purity, and integrity?

I Peter 3:12 states, *For the eyes of the Lord are upon the righteous (those who are upright and in right standing with God), and His ears are attentive to their prayer. But the face of the Lord is against those who practice evil [to oppose them, to frustrate, and defeat them]. (Amplified Bible)*

Righteousness and holiness are signs of a pure heart. The Lord is specific about those who are walking uprightly before Him. His eyes are upon those who are righteous and holy, and His ears are listening to those prayers prayed by righteous and holy lips! Who would not want the Lord to be watching and listening when we pray?

Integrity of worship is fruitful worship. Fruitful worship is worship that remains long past the "amen" of a particular service. Fruitful worship is fruit that remains long after the music has stopped, the praying has finished, and all the people have gone home. Fruitful worship remains even after the season is passing. When Jesus comes and examines our lives because He is hungry for our worship will He find any remaining fruit on us? He will on me.

Let's look again at Mark 11:12-14.

Now the next day, when they had come out from Bethany, He was hungry.
And seeing from afar a fig tree having leaves, He went to see if perhaps He would find something on it. When He came to it, He found nothing but leaves, for it was not the season for figs. In response Jesus said to it, "Let no one eat fruit from you ever again." And His disciples heard it.

I grew up in the south where fig trees are abundant. The climate is right and they live a very long time. The fig tree is unique from all other fruit trees. The fig tree 'fruits' first, then later on it produces leaves. The fruit will remain while the leaves gradually grow out. The actual fruit is for giving. The leaves are for receiving sunlight, nutrients, moisture, etc. Fig trees give fruit first, then receive what is needed to sustain them. When Jesus saw the fig tree having leaves, He went to find fruit to eat. But there was no fruit.

Jesus never cursed the fig tree. The disciples said that He did, but if you read the words Jesus said to the tree, He did not curse it. He merely sealed it in its fruitlessness. It was fruitless when fruit should have still remained, so He sealed it in its present condition. To be sealed forever in a fruitless condition would be beyond anything I could ever withstand or comprehend. It should be more than you could take too. It must have been more than the fig tree could take too, for within twenty-four hours the tree had begun to wither up and die. Why? The tree had lost its purpose. The tree's purpose was to give fruit first, then grow leaves for receiving, while continuing to give fruit. Being sealed in a non-purposeful condition caused the tree to wither and die.

Like the fig tree, none of us can live without our God-given purpose being fulfilled within us. When we are not doing and being who we were created to be, then we begin to wither up and die. We have something the fig tree did not have though. As long as we have a breath within us we can make a choice to change, to be different and to produce fruit. When Jesus comes looking around in your life, lifting your leaves and looking underneath for fruit that remains, will He be able to be fed from your first fruits that continue and remain? He should be! If not, you can change today.

So we are not simply representing our own names, keeping our own names clean and pure before Him, we are representing His name. People don't want the responsibility but nonetheless, we have it. What responsibility is that? We hold the responsibility of keeping God's name to the highest of levels of integrity. How can we do this? Not by living perfect, because we cannot do that. It is impossible for any human other than Jesus Christ, the son of God to live perfectly. So how do we uphold and protect His name with integrity? We do it by living our lives honestly, and openly. We should never try to hide our failures, but rather in exposing them through repentance, that in itself causes us to keep our "act" cleaned up.

I remember as a late teenager, I fell deeply in love with Jesus. I began to realize what it truly means to live for Him. I began to cherish each and every moment I was given to feel His presence and be with Him. Like all humans, I had my own faults. And being a musician and a called worshiper, I had the normal human faults and then the higher levels of temptations that it seems only worshipers fall so prey to. I began to feel defeated every day as I would try so hard not to fall to temptation but could not seem to get through even one whole day without my pride rising up, without my own desire to be seen and heard above all others. I would spend much time each night in my prayer time repenting and knowing that once again I had failed my precious Lord with my own desires and pleasure-seeking through pride.

The Lord told me in prayer one night that He did not want me to come to Him the following night and repent and be sorry any more. I was confused at first, and then He went on to explain. He told me that I had been given more than enough time to grow up in this area and that His requirement for me was to immediately repent. No matter who I was with, no matter in what situation or circumstance I would find myself, if I failed to give Him the glory due His name and for whatever reason I fed my own pride, selfishness, or self-focused promotion, I must repent in front of whomever was present! Wow, this seemed quite harsh and more than a little bit hard! But I knew this was not a request but a command from the Lord.

The following day, I did not get very far into the first hour of my day until I fell prey to the temptation of self-promotion. The Holy Spirit reminded me that I must immediately repent, and He meant right now! I was so embarrassed and even ashamed, but I obeyed the Lord. I embarrassed myself and confessed this hidden desire of my heart to be lifted up. Most of my immediate friends were standing there and they just stared at me like I had lost my mind. None of my friends in high school had experienced the same encounter with the Lord so they already thought I was a bit different, quite strange and peculiar; well, truthfully, I think they all thought I was just plain weird. After my abrupt confession of my self-pride, my friends just looked at me and did not say one word. But I was changed, right then and there. I was held accountable to that level to live and be a worshiper of integrity. I never forgot that humiliation.

The next time my flesh wanted to self-promote and my heart had the desire to be lifted up, it did not go unnoticed by my spirit man. I learned the hard way the cost of hidden pride; once the Lord required me to repent in front of everybody I quickly became sensitive to the Holy Spirit more to help me! I am not saying that I did not sin in this area again, I did, and I had to follow it up with humiliating confessions of my heart's hidden self-desires in front of all present. It took a while, and quite a bit of embarrassment but I finally understood the cost of being who God has called me to be. I finally understood to stand in His presence with my integrity intact it would cost me every hidden motive and intention of my heart.

We never truly arrive as long as we are housed in these flesh-suits but we can certainly help our spirit to become stronger than our flesh. It's a journey that will cost you everything you thought valuable at one time in your life. But once you pay the price, you will realize as I did, that what seemed most valuable in my sight had absolutely no value in His presence. So what we give Him may not be of any value to Him, but it costs us everything, and like David spoke from his heart when he said that he would not give to God what cost him nothing, neither shall I.

Your integrity retained is a journey that never ends on this earth. So stay on the path of righteousness and holiness hidden within His presence. You can retain your integrity and hopefully, be around long enough to talk about it to the next generation of worshipers.

In Genesis 32, God changed Jacob's name because Jacob finally wrestled with God long enough and hard enough to leave God's mark on his life. When Jacob was changed in his character and his integrity, then God changed his name. Jacob's name was changed because his destiny was changed. When God gives us a new name it is because *"old things are passed away and all things have become new."* Once we are on the accountable, correctable, path of integrity then our name reflects our destiny. *"A good name is better than precious ointment."* A good name reflects your path, your journey and your destination.

I finally understood to stand in His presence with my integrity intact, it would cost me every hidden motive and intention of my heart.

Chapter Nine Questions:

1. Have I completely taken the name of Jesus Christ as my own Bridegroom?

____

____

____

____

2. In taking His name, am I honoring and protecting that name in my actions and choices?

____

____

____

____

3. Do I truly know His name and all that the name of Jesus Christ entails?

____

____

____

____

4. Does He know my name?

____

____

____

____

____

5. Name the signs of a pure heart.

____

____

____

____

____

6. When is worship "fruitful?"

7. Am I being fruitful, producing and fulfilling my God-given purpose?

8. What responsibility have I been given, if I am a true worshiper of Christ and have taken His name as my Bridegroom?

9. As a musician, do I recognize that my talents come only from God and am I giving Him His due glory, or am I keeping some for myself?

10. What will it cost me to retain godly integrity?

Chapter Ten
An Accountable Worshiper

Many times we don't realize what is stopping the true flow of worship in our lives. The Bible says in Matthew 5:23-24, *Therefore if you bring your gift to the altar, and there remember that your brother has something against you, leave your gift there before the altar, and go your way. First be reconciled to your brother, and then come and offer your gift.*

This particular scripture covers some things that I like to call "permissive sins." We hold on to particular happenings, words spoken, personality differences, etc. many times to the point that we have lost relationship with people the Lord has specifically put in our lives. There are moments when this has happened merely because of immature, self-centered, and self-focused Christians. I am talking about Christians now, not those who *say* they are Christians, but truly those who have given their lives to Jesus Christ and call Him Lord. But because our society is so mirror-imaged based we can miss the bigger picture.

We pretend like this scripture in Matthew is not even in the Bible. We don't want to have to be accountable for our actions, or our attitudes toward others. Some of the very people that we spend holidays avoiding are people we also pray to spend eternity with! We want them to go to heaven, but preferably not in our heavenly neighborhoods! We pray they spend eternity with Jesus but not eternity with us! What kind of selfish attitudes am I speaking of here? I am talking about the kinds of attitudes that can keep the Lord from receiving our gifts at the altar!

We read this passage and I don't know about you, but I have always thought the "gift" in reference here was my monetary gift. But we bring many gifts to the altar of the Lord. We are to bring our gifts and talents to the altar in worship. When we bring our gifts, talents, and hearts of worship to Him, and we have ought against our brother, the Lord is specific as to the steps we are to take in our presentation.

First, we are to leave our gift right there at the altar. If we leave our gift at the altar then we cannot use that gift, give that gift, benefit from that gift, or receive a harvest from that gift until we first make peace with our brother. Then, we can come back and present our gift to the Lord! Can you imagine that when we have problems with other people in the body of Christ, our very brothers and sisters in Christ that the Lord says our gifts are of no value to Him until we first make peace with one another! Just from this circumstance and situation alone, we can see why so many churches are filled with so-called worship services that are nothing of worship at all! They are rituals, religious at best, but not worship, not worship in spirit and truth!

Please don't misunderstand me. I am not saying that we have to like everybody, or get along with everybody, or agree with everybody in the entire body of Christ for our gifts to be received by the Lord. We all know this is not going to happen. We can't even agree on basic fundamental principles within the body of Christ! Doctrines are always going to be roadblocks to our agreement but are they also roadblocks to our worship? Should we maybe be looking for those things we can agree upon instead of focusing on those continual points of dissention?

But this is not what the Lord is concerned with in our lives of worship. He is concerned with our hearts and with those people who are in our lives regularly. We are not to be coming before the Lord when we have not even taken the time and effort to work out as many things between those around us as possible. After thirty years of evangelistic ministry, we have heard almost every possible scenario of worshipers who do not get along, who are jealous, covetous, resentful and bitter towards one another. Yet they step up on the platform to "worship" the Lord when love is not even flowing between the members of the team! So how can love flow toward God when it does not even flow on the platform?

Many years ago, I saw a vision of an entire congregation in powerful worship. The Lord showed me that His fire was upon each head. The fire of the Lord was causing smoke to rise from each worshiper. As it rose higher and higher, the smoke began to come together swirling over the heads of all the worshipers, causing the heads of each individual worshiper to no longer be able to be seen. From heaven's view, the mingling of the smoke and the fragrance of each worshiper, ever spiraling upward toward the throne of God, became one huge fragrant worshiper. For the first time I understood why those who have already tapped into the intimate places of worship can worship with those who have no idea how to overcome their own minds and thoughts. As the worship began to rise higher and higher, it covered those who had not yet fully understood the truth and spirit of God's kind of worship. But because they were willing to just "be there," with pure hearts and motives, they were included in the entire whole of worship.

God received their worship at the level they were ready to give it and the fragrance of it all intermingled together was so beautifully refreshing to the Lord. In the vision, I actually saw the Lord smile as if to say how pleased He was with those who know how to enter in, and with those who even though did not know yet, were still willing to get involved. Just by getting into the worship, they were learning how to become worship!

This accountability of leaving our gifts at the altar and going and making peace with a brother or sister is part of the service of an accountable worshiper and it is being required.

The Lord specifically says that the way we treat others can hinder our prayers, and even our giving at His altar. I would think it very important that we stop pretending these things do not matter, or even worse, we justify our heart's offenses; places filled with bitterness, and get these things taken care of in our hearts. The Lord knows.

> *I will make peace with my brothers and sisters.*

The enemy's roadblock to worship is broken relationships. God's way to enter in to His presence is broken pride, broken lives, and broken hearts. This leaves nothing of "self" left in us.

Hebrews 13:17 is one of the best scriptures on submission and accountability in the entire Bible. It is quite simple as it states, *Obey your spiritual leaders and submit to them [continually recognizing their authority over you], for they are constantly keeping watch over your souls and guarding your spiritual welfare, as men who will have to render an account [of their trust]. [Do your part to] let them do this with gladness and not with sighing and groaning, for that would not be profitable to you [either]. (Amplified Bible)*

One of the biggest problems in organized church is that many times the pastor in the church has to "pastor and shepherd" worshipers who are so controlled by the luciferian spirit of pride, that every worship service is all about the worshipers and not about the One who is being worshiped. Many pastors are not prepared for this huge pride thing that goes on in the hearts and lives of some musicians. I cannot tell you how many times we have seen pastors discouraged by trying to keep their worshipers happy. I believe God is more interested in our being holy than He is in our being happy.

The mother in me wants to take them all out back to the woodshed and kick the "pride" right out of them! But I know that is not what I have been called to do, but still that is my first thought! When worship is about the worshiper and not about the Lord there is no way to fix this. It might as well get thrown out completely! We might as well start all over, for a little leaven will spoil the whole lump! It might seem harsh to say but it is truthful. Pride is infectious like a disease and once it is tolerated and not held to accountability, then it is time to throw it all out and do without for a period of time. The Lord knows the hearts and He knows that too many pastors have been held hostage by pride-filled worship leaders who threaten to leave over this "thing" or that "whatever."

May it not be so any more, Lord! May we have the courage to stand up to pride and expose it. For the souls of those called to worship to be cleansed and purified through repentance and brokenness at Your feet. May Your worship be restored to the spirit and truth, highest level that You deserve!

As worshipers, we are accountable first to the Holy Spirit, and then to those in authority over us in this natural realm. We need to learn to be held accountable. We need to learn to pull our flesh under when we feel it get "pinched." When our egos are not stroked to the level in which we are accustomed, or our way is not always the one which is followed, we need to learn to give in! We need it!

It is so good for us to have to bend and be flexible! Why? Because we are going to stand in the high office of worshiper and we need to have had much time practicing in the realm of submission. To be led of the spirit is the only way we can be a true worshiper. For how can we worship in spirit and in truth if we do not submit and become continually, literally every moment, accountable to the Holy Ghost?

What I want you to understand is that when we have anything in our hearts against anyone, it can cause us to not be able to enter into God's presence. By forgiving and making peace with any and all people it is not a get out of jail free card to those who have hurt us repeatedly. It is not an excuse or permission for anyone to purposely do and say those things to us that hurt and wound our hearts. With all things in the presence of God, it is not what has happened to us, but how we react to what has happened. It is not what others have done, but how we have reacted to what others have done to us. We will never stand before God in judgment over what someone else chooses to do or not to do. But we will stand in judgment over our own responses and reactions to everything that happens in us, to us, and around us.

God's way
to enter into
His presence
is *broken pride, broken lives,*
and *broken hearts.*

Chapter Ten Questions:

1. What is one thing that can stop the flow of worship in my life?

____
____
____
____
____
____

2. What does the scripture in Matthew 5:23-24 tell me to do in this case?

____
____
____
____
____
____

3. What is the Lord most concerned with in our worship lives?

____
____
____
____
____
____

4. As it relates to this chapter, what one word describes the humbling action of leaving my gift at the altar in order to go and make peace with a brother, and then returning to the altar to present that gift to the Lord?

____

5. What is the enemy's roadblock to worship?

6. What is God's entry way for us into His presence?

7. What is the only way to be a true worshiper?

8. It is good for musicians, worshipers and all in the body of Christ to learn submission. Why?

Chapter Eleven
A Submissive Worshiper

Ephesians 5:19-21
Speak out to one another in psalms and hymns and spiritual songs, offering praise with voices [and instruments] and making melody with all your heart to the Lord, at all times and for everything giving thanks in the name of our Lord Jesus Christ to God the Father. Be subject to one another out of reverence for Christ (the Messiah, the Anointed One). (Amplified Bible)

I submit to You, Lord!

Submission is one of the most powerful tools of the power of agreement. Agreement is a necessary ingredient to powerful worship. Submission must be a heart practice. It must become a way of life for the worshiper. One must above all things submit to the Holy Spirit, for how can we ever worship Him in spirit and truth without the leading and directing of the One who is spirit and truth?

So a worshiper's first level of defense is submission to the Holy Spirit. This can only come at the feet of our Lord and Master. We give Him our gifts, talents, minds, wills and emotions. We give Him our program, our performance and our preparation. We give Him our abilities and our inabilities. We give Him our plans. We lay our thoughts and ideas and then ultimately our selves at His feet. We submit and commit to be still, to listen, and then to obey.

Once we have obtained His divine connection through our choice to submit to Him fully, then the next level of submission must be obtained. Worshipers, musicians, dancers, all of us seen on the platform, or in any part of the worship service must submit to the authority of a church -

the pastor, the appointed shepherd of the church. If we cannot submit to an earthly shepherd, how can we submit to our heavenly Shepherd? If we are to be 'one' in His presence, then we must learn to be 'one' in His pulpit and on His platform. Learning to listen, follow instructions, and obey is a huge part of trusting God and each other to flow by His spirit.

True worshipers must operate in yet another level of submission. What possible level of submission is this? We must submit to one another. Why? The Bible tells us to submit to one another, using Philippians 2:2-3 as a basis for the power of God's amazing tools to be unleashed in our personal worship and our corporate worship.

...fulfill my joy by being like-minded, having the same love, being of one accord, of one mind. Let nothing be done through selfish ambition or conceit, but in lowliness of mind let each esteem others better than himself.

It's time to learn and understand that the true flow of worship becomes much more powerful as we intermingle our giftings and callings, not one person being seen or heard, but the power of One, the power of the legal summons of God's presence through agreement and submitting to one another. Learning to put oneself aside and help the others to get ahead, thinking more highly of others than of ourselves, this is God's way.

In Isaiah 6:1-2, we can see three elements of worship being outlined.

In the year that King Uzziah died, I saw the Lord sitting on a throne, high and lifted up, and the train of His robe filled the temple. Above it stood seraphim; each one had six wings: with two he covered his face, with two he covered his feet, and with two he flew.

The seraphim had six wings. These wings were used in sets of two. There were two used to cover their faces, which represents their reverence toward the Lord and His throne. There were two used to cover their feet as they bowed down in adoration and submission. Then there were two for flying in obedience and service for the Lord Most High! From the seraphim, we can see three very important elements of worship: 1. Reverence 2. Adoring submission 3. Obedience

As His worshipers, we must constantly keep ourselves in a repentant state of mind and heart. We must never lose our reverent fear of the Lord or misunderstand the magnitude of this position to which we have been called. We must never take it lightly that we have been chosen and allowed to walk in this office before His throne.

As His worshipers, we must never think that it is about us, for it is not about us, and it never will be! It is about Him and Him only, forever and ever! He deserves to be adored; if you do not adore our Lord, long for Him more than anything else on the earth, then move over and get out of the way. The Lord is only looking for those who adore Him.

As His worshipers, we must obey Him at all times. We do not belong to ourselves anymore. We do not belong to our own hopes or dreams or desires of flesh. We do not belong to our soul realms, our feelings or emotions. We belong only to Him and for Him. God deserves reverence, adoration and obedience. If you are not willing to give these things, there are many for whom His eyes are searching the earth… who are! You and I are not important here, only He is! If you won't do the job to the level it must be done, then stop taking up space on the platform of the altar of worship before the King of kings. He will fill your spot quickly; He will find the one who will worship Him in spirit and truth.

He is not willing to do without reverent, submitted, and obedient worship.

Colossians 3:16-17 gives us a clear picture of what our worship should be toward one another. It is a practical way we can be using our gifts for His glory.

Let the word [spoken by] Christ (the Messiah) have its home [in your hearts and minds] and dwell in you in [all its] richness, as you teach and admonish and train one another in all insight and intelligence and wisdom, [in spiritual things, and as you sing] psalms and hymns and spiritual songs, making melody to God with [His] grace in your hearts. And whatever you do [no matter what it is] in word or deed, do everything in the name of the Lord Jesus and in [dependence upon] His Person, giving praise to God the Father through Him. (Amplified Bible)

We are supposed to use our gifts and talents of music in our communication between each other as we sing psalms and hymns and spiritual songs. We are to make melodies to God in our hearts! I long to see this generation of worshipers turn loose of the spirit of performance that dominated and paralyzed the true flow of worship in my generation. Performance has been exposed as the true thief that it is. The demonic spirits of performance, perfectionism and approval have for too long stolen the truth and spirit of God's worship. No more! These three demonic strongholds have been exposed and called out by the Holy Ghost within us! We are not allowing it any longer! God is on His throne and we are not! It is not about us, never has been, and never will be! He must be lifted up!

Psalm 100:1-2
Make a joyful noise unto the Lord, all you lands! Serve the Lord with gladness! Come before His presence with singing! (Amplified Bible)

Whether our gifts are the greatest by the world's standards is not important to the Lord. His desire for worship is to have it in spirit and truth. The greatest gifts may be used on the stage for the world's applause and accolades but the Lord is not impressed! He will raise up worshipers! The greatest gifts were created for His pleasure but if they are not given back to that magnificent purpose, and instead are flaunted for worldly, cheering crowds, He will continue to search the entire earth over for those who will worship Him in spirit and in truth.

Can you see the thread that continues to weave the most beautiful and intricate of all tapestries before the Lord? It is not about talent. It is not about natural beauty, or the measures of the world's standards of gifts and talents. With God it always has been and it always will be about the heart.

It is not about the strength of the mind or the will of a person. It is about how well we are submitted to the power of the Holy Spirit within us. We must learn to yield our entire beings to the Spirit of God if we truly want to be worship before Him.

I Corinthians 14:15 answers the question of spirit worship and its place in the body of Christ and in particular in our daily lives. Paul addressed the question and the use of the gift of tongues within the gathering of many people.

Then what am I to do? I will pray with my spirit [by the Holy Spirit that is within me], but I will also pray [intelligently] with my mind and understanding; I will sing with my spirit [by the Holy Spirit that is within me], but I will sing [intelligently] with my mind and understanding also. (Amplified Bible)

Never misinterpret this to mean that the Holy Spirit is not

intelligent! For the things of the Spirit are far beyond the comprehension of our lower, slower earthly minds. This *Amplified Bible* translation is merely making the distinction between what is understood by the mind of humanity versus the things far beyond human comprehension. Our intellect can only grasp the things of this world. We cannot, even with the greatest of human minds, begin to scratch the surface of the lowest level of understanding in the Spirit of God.

When I pray and fellowship with the Lord because I love to worship, music is an easy way for me to quickly enter into His presence. But as I have matured in the Lord He has taken me through seasons where He has required me to come before Him without the "help" of the streams of the rivers of prerecorded music. He wants me to come before Him with singing! What does He want me to sing? He wants me to sing the song of the redeemed! He wants me to sing from my heart a love song that only He and I have between us! He wants me to sing of my adoration and longing for Him. He wants to hear my intellectual interpretations of songs that my mind can comprehend and then when I run out of my own language and it is too inadequate to express my heart towards Him, then He wants me to rely on the Holy Spirit within me to sing a new song to Him that only He can interpret! He knows me! He knows my mind, my heart and only He knows my spirit! My spirit belongs solely to Him! He alone can understand who He has created me to be!

Submission is the main ingredient for multiple of worshipers to be able to worship at His throne. When we are submitted to His will then we can flow by His Spirit and the great Conductor can orchestrate even the very sounds coming forth from our beings in perfect harmony and unity. Many can operate as a unified being of worship when submission is in operation and the Spirit of God is in full control.

I see by my spirit into the near future where many can worship the Lord in spirit and truth. I see the ebb and flow of the River of Life pouring forth through many worshipers. Songs come forth flowing like a cleansing and purifying river from one voice, then another, then at the same time. I see musicians, dancers, singers all operating as one, in unity and perfect harmony as if much preparation has been made in advance, much practice has gone forth. Yet, there has been absolutely no time spent in preparation with each other. Only at His feet in prayerful submission has each worshiper been molded, tested and tried in His presence causing each piece of the worshipers puzzle to be cut perfectly to fit together as the most beautiful mosaic of all time. It is in the perfection of each piece at His feet that causes the beauty of the whole to be so magnificent. He is the great Creator, the ultimate Conductor, the master Sculptor who can take the simplest of each piece, individual worshipers, but when molded and melted together into one masterpiece by His hands, become the highest of all worship and praise, truth and spirit yielded before Him… purest worship… purest sounds of His presence.

> Submission *is one of the most* powerful tools *of the power of agreement.* Submission *must be a* heart *practice.*

Chapter Eleven Questions:

1. ______________________ is a powerful part of ______________________, which is a necessary ingredient to powerful worship.

2. True worshipers must first be submissive to ______________________.

3. The next level of submission for the true worshiper is to ______________________.

4. The next level of submission for the true worshiper is to ______________________.

4. As His worshipers, we must constantly keep ourselves in a ______________________ state of mind and heart.

5. Name three things that have stolen the truth and spirit of God's worship.

    1.
    2.
    3.

6. With God, it (worship, talents and gifts) always has been and it always will be about ______________________.

7. ______________________ is the main ingredient for multiple worshipers to be able to worship at His throne, in harmony.

Chapter Twelve
An Authoritative/Disciplined Worshiper

Proverbs 29:2
When the righteous are in authority, the people rejoice; but when a wicked man rules, the people groan.

Matthew 28:18-20
And Jesus came and spoke to them, saying, "All authority has been given to Me in heaven and on earth. Go therefore and make disciples of all the nations, baptizing them in the name of the Father and of the Son and of the Holy Spirit, teaching them to observe all things that I have commanded you; and lo, I am with you always, even to the end of the age." Amen.

John 17:1-5
Jesus spoke these words, lifted up His eyes to heaven, and said: "Father, the hour has come. Glorify Your Son, that Your Son also may glorify You, as You have given Him authority over all flesh, that He should give eternal life to as many as You have given Him. And this is eternal life, that they may know You, the only true God, and Jesus Christ whom You have sent. I have glorified You on the earth. I have finished the work which You have given Me to do. And now, O Father, glorify Me together with Yourself, with the glory which I had with You before the world was."

I rejoice, knowing who I am in Christ!

Authority is a powerful tool in the hands of the right people. When righteous people are in authority it is cause for rejoicing! All authority has been given to Jesus according to the passage of scripture in Matthew 28. Then this statement is followed by Jesus Christ, with all authority sending out those who will yield to His authority, making disciples of all the nations! We are being sent forth not in our own strength and not alone! We are being sent forth with the all authoritative One going with us, as He promised that He is with us always, even to the end of the age! We don't have to operate in our own authority or strength but in His authority and strength!

Once we realize that this entire earth journey is not about us, what we can gain or achieve, but in Christ Jesus we can accomplish the mission in which we are sent forth to be and do, then and only then can we rejoice and be glad! As we long to know more and do more, we must learn that it is in our patience and endurance at His feet that we can receive the glory of His presence that transforms us, mere human beings, into the glorious expressions of who He is!

I Kings 8:10-24
And it came to pass, when the priests came out of the holy place, that the cloud filled the house of the Lord, so that the priests could not continue ministering because of the cloud; for the glory of the Lord filled the house of the Lord. Then Solomon spoke: "The Lord said He would dwell in the dark cloud. I have surely built You an exalted house, and a place for You to dwell in forever."

Then the king turned around and blessed the whole assembly of Israel, while all the assembly of Israel was standing. And he said; "Blessed be the Lord God of Israel, who spoke with His mouth to my father David, and with His hand has fulfilled it, saying, 'Since the day that I brought My people Israel out of Egypt, I have chosen no city from any tribe of Israel in which to build a house, that My name might be there; but I chose David to be over My people Israel.'

"Now it was in the heart of my father David to build a temple for the name of the Lord God of Israel. But the Lord said to my father David, 'Whereas it was in your heart to build a temple for My name, you did well that it was in your heart. Nevertheless you shall not build the temple, but your son who will come from your body, he shall build the temple for My name.'

"So the Lord has fulfilled His word which He spoke; and I have filled the position of my father David, and sit on the throne of Israel, as the Lord promised; and I have built a temple for the name of the Lord God of Israel. And there I have made a place for the ark, in which is the covenant of the Lord which He made with our fathers, when He brought them out of the land of Egypt."

Then Solomon stood before the altar of the Lord in the presence of all the assembly of Israel, and spread out his hands toward heaven; and he said: "Lord God of Israel, there is no God in heaven above or on earth below like You, who keep Your covenant and mercy with Your servants who walk before You with all their hearts. You have kept what You promised Your servant David my father; You have both spoken with Your mouth and fulfilled it with Your hand, as it is this day."

Through the Word of God, we have been given His authority. It comes through understanding and knowing who we truly are inside of Him. It comes through understanding the power of His commitment to us by giving us His name. His name represents His authority, so once we have a name change, a destiny change, then we also have an authority level change. We are no longer living in the authority of our own lives and names but in His!

Authority is not about power, but about His presence. Authority is not about who is in charge but who is responsible. Authority is not about who is on top but rather who is willing to take the blame when necessary. Authority is not about being #1, but about being submitted to #1. Authority is not about commanding respect but about being respectful. Authority is not about demanding anything but about submitting to the outcome of all things. Authority is not about a position, but about a commission. Authority is not about knowing what to say, but about knowing when not to say anything.

God's positioning of our lives at His feet is giving us the opportunity to bow to His authority by our own will and choice. When we are willing to lower ourselves to the lowest possible point at His feet, then and only then can we be used to our highest abilities through His highest authority.

Luke 4:6-7
And the devil said to Him, "All this authority I will give You, and their glory; for this has been delivered to me, and I give it to whomever I wish. Therefore, if You will worship before me, all will be Yours."

This scripture is almost comical if it were not so sad. The fallen angel of worship, Lucifer, now referred to as Satan or the devil in this particular passage of scripture was trying to tempt Jesus Christ, God's own Son through the dangling of the carrot of authority. What's so amazing is that the devil is so delusional by this point in his demise that he must have convinced himself that he actually had some authority to present to the Messiah, the Christ! Of course, he had no authority at all. Notice how he worded this so-called authority. *"For this (authority) has been delivered to me,"* the devil stated to Jesus. How deceived the devil was by his own pride to presume that he had any authority at all! We must be so cautious to not be deceived by our own pride to think that we actually have anything to give back to the Creator of the universe! All that we have to give to Him is what we have been given authority over, which is the destiny of our future. Our eternal future has been given into our own hands by the fall of mankind into sin. This and only this is what we have to give back to God.

We can willfully give back to God our future. I must choose, and so must you, where we will spend eternity. I give my life, my future, all my abilities and inabilities to My eternal Lord and King. I pray for the Lord to illuminate my eternal spiritual eyes so that I can see what is truly real and also what is delusional and deceptive. I ask the Lord to discipline us and disciple us. I ask the Lord to open our eyes and help us stay focused on the true light of His presence. I ask the Lord to use me to help open the eyes of the deceived, appointed worshipers of our generation through the light and truth of His presence. I strip off my old nature and walk in the Spirit even as He is in the Spirit moving ever so carefully into the eternal paths of glory, disciplined and authoritative, secure in Him, who loves me.

"Discipline" means "making disciples." When we hear the word discipline we must not cringe away as if it is the ultimate of pain! Discipline is the journey of becoming a disciple of Christ. To become Christ-like we must learn how to embrace discipline and love this correction of the Spirit of God in our lives.

Do you want to be loved by the Lord? *Whom the Lord loves He corrects!* (Proverbs 3:12) Then in Proverbs 12:1, *Whoever loves instruction loves knowledge, but he who hates correction is stupid.* Okay, so let me ask the question again. Do you want the Lord to love you? If your answer is yes, then you must also love His instruction and His correction. This is the Lord teaching and training us to become His disciples.

Elisha was a great prophet; he took over when Elijah left in the chariot of fire from the Lord. Elisha followed Elijah around until he saw him taken up into heaven, getting Elijah's mantle and taking it upon himself as a sign of the anointing of God passing from one man to another. Elisha was used to being trained and disciplined as he had submitted himself to Elijah.

When Elisha was summoned to appear before the king of Israel he did not want to go, nor did he want to give the king a word from the Lord. In fact, he said to the king, "*What have I to do with you? Go to the prophets of your father and the prophets of your mother.*" (II Kings 3:13).

The king of Israel, the king of Judah, and the king of Edom began to realize that God was about to deliver them into the hand of Moab. King Jehoshaphat asked if there was not a prophet of God anywhere around through whom they could consult God? One of the servants spoke up and said that Elisha son of Shaphat was around there somewhere, and went on to explain that Elisha had taken over for Elijah. Jehoshaphat thought this a great idea and felt the three kings could trust Elisha to be a true prophet.

This is where we pick up the story of what Elisha did at this point. He obviously did not want to be used by the Lord to help these three kings. He did not like these kings calling for him; he may not have felt like the hand of the Lord was upon him at that moment. Have you ever been in that place? Where you are being called upon to "be anointed" and you just don't feel it?

The Bible gives us a clear path of understanding in the

following verses using what Elisha did to receive the anointing from the Lord.

II Kings 3:14-15
And Elisha said, "As the Lord of hosts lives, before whom I stand, surely were it not that I regard the presence of Jehoshaphat king of Judah, I would not look at you, nor see you. But now bring me a musician." Then it happened, when the musician played, that the hand of the Lord came upon him.

Even a single note can move us into the presence of Almighty God. Even a single line of melody can be like a mighty rushing river taking us to the very feet of our Lord! Elisha understood this concept; he had most probably used this method to get into the flow of the anointing of the Lord before. I can almost hear him let out a long and slow sigh as he said for them to bring him a musician.

Let this be a warning to you though, if you are a musician. As musicians, we must be careful to only use the gifts the Lord has given us for His glory and under His commands. Music is a powerful sound wave on this earth. It can change the mood of people and atmospheres of gatherings. Music can calm the nerves, bringing the soul under control, or stir up the spirit to the point that entire nations will go to war all driven by the sound wave of a beating drum!

Music is a powerful tool in the hands and heart of a disciplined worshiper. But without the deepest of relationships with our Creator, music can be used to bring about selfish motives and fulfill man's desires instead of God's will. We, as musical worshipers, must guard against the temptation to use our gifts in services and gatherings without the leading of the Holy Spirit.

In the scripture in II Kings, we see Elisha the prophet calling for a musician to come and play. Why? Because when the musician played, Elisha could access the move of the Spirit of God quickly in his spirit. Music is like waves on the ocean. It can either carry you safely to the shore or the riptide forces of it can pull you so quickly away from safety, that without warning you are in the middle of the ocean surrounded by sharks!

We must be careful to spend much time praying in the Spirit if we expect the Lord to use us with our musical gifts for His glory. We must continually be yielded to His presence and not allow our soul realms to direct our paths. Where the Lord leads we may not want to follow. It may not be the pleasant path but rather the "road less traveled." We must stay in constant communication with the Spirit of God so we don't make our own way, led by our emotions and desires.

A gift in the area of music, whether singing, playing an instrument, or dance is given to a person to be given back to the Lord in praise and worship. This beautiful gift is for His glory revealed in the life of the one who receives it. Anything less than this can be defiling the gift within the musician. We who are musical must guard our hearts and minds even more than any other worshiper because of the temptation of pride and self-adoration. The Bible has laid out in clear detail to us how to safeguard against this self-destructive pattern of pride.

In Ezekiel 28, an account of the demise of Lucifer is recounted. Lucifer was the chief worshiper in heaven. He was in charge of the worship. He was included in the rank of the sons of God in the Book of Job 1:6, *Now there was a day when the sons of God came to present themselves before the Lord, and Satan also came among them.* Whether Lucifer was ever referred to as one of the sons of God is definitely in question. But we know by this scripture that even in his fallen state as Satan, he was presumptuous. For when the sons of God presented themselves before the Lord, he came too! Pride goes before a fall and we see here that it stays with you after the fall also!

In Ezekiel 28:12-19, the story begins of Lucifer, before the sin of pride took root in him, as the Lord God explains the progression of his demise.

You were the seal of perfection, full of wisdom and perfect in beauty.

You were in Eden, the garden of God; every precious stone was your covering: the sardius, topaz, and diamond, beryl, onyx, and jasper, sapphire, turquoise, and emerald with gold. The workmanship of your timbrels and pipes was prepared for you on the day you were created.

You were the anointed cherub who covers; I established you; You were on the holy mountain of God; you walked back and forth in the midst of fiery stones. You were perfect in your ways from the day you were created, till iniquity was found in you.

By the abundance of your trading you were filled with violence from within, and you sinned; therefore I cast you as a profane thing out of the mountain of God; and I destroyed you, O covering cherub, from the midst of the fiery stones.

Your heart was lifted up because of your beauty; you corrupted your wisdom for the sake of your splendor; I cast you to the ground, I laid you before kings that they might gaze at you.

You defiled your sanctuaries by the multitude of your iniquities, by the iniquity of your trading; therefore I brought fire from your midst; it devoured you, and I turned you to ashes upon the earth in the sight of all who saw you.

All who knew you among the peoples are astonished at you; you have become a horror, and shall be no more forever.

Verse 17 in the *Message Bible* reads, *Your beauty went to your head. You corrupted wisdom by using it to get worldly fame.*

In the thirty years I have been in full time ministry, I have watched the rise and fall of many anointed worshipers because of their giftings and talents going to their head. As each one wanted worldly fame more than they wanted to please God, I have seen the downward spiral of these precious gifts have to be thrown out of the kingdom of God just as Lucifer had to be.

This position of worshiper in the kingdom has to be guarded more than any other. It's as if the worshipers are the peacocks in the animal kingdom. We have to guard against strutting around showing off our feathers! We have been given the gifts and callings we possess simply for His pleasure, His glory, His honor and His worship! Any portion of our gift used to bring us "worldly fame" is a distortion of our gifts and is the beginning of our own downfall.

It cannot be "played with." You cannot be so prideful as to think you are strong enough on your own to protect this gift. You are not strong enough! It is only through the bowing of our knees at His feet, the lifting of our hands toward His throne, and the yielding of our self-willed pride, to His Spirit, that can we survive this temptation. We must learn to yield to Him, through much prayer and fasting, through submission and accountability to those the Lord puts over us in authority.

Lucifer was the chief musician in heaven! He had access to the fiery stones on the mountain of God! But his heart became lifted up with his own abilities, gifts, and beauty. This pride cost him his future in the kingdom of God. Do not go down the same road of prideful destruction and lose your God-given position within the kingdom! And if you are thinking that this would never happen to you, then you should tremble at His feet at this very moment for you are next in line to be tempted!

Not only can it happen to you, but it will happen to you! This kind of prideful temptation will happen to us all, and the one who thinks he or she would never fall to this is standing in line to walk off the cliff! Who are you and I to ever think that we could not be tempted, when our Lord, Jesus Himself was tempted by Satan! Of course, He withstood that temptation, but He is the only One who has ever walked this earth without spot or wrinkle and without sin.

Even in our thoughts of "this could never happen to me," pride is ever present! Cleanse your minds and hearts with repentance, submission, and accountability even now! I urge you to get on your face and ask the Lord to strengthen you through the power of the Holy Spirit. Pray, pray, pray with the Spirit of God helping our weaknesses and keeping sin from taking root in our midst.

It takes great discipline to keep our hearts and minds in check before the Lord. It takes a constant understanding that we can never arrive to a place of no temptation until we leave these bodies behind. Lucifer was not in a physical flesh body and yet he was lifted up and pride-filled! We must be so careful to protect our minds and hearts by the infilling of the Holy Spirit and the leading of His wisdom keeping us clean before Him.

When we are willing to lower ourselves to the lowest possible point at His feet, *then and only then can we be used to our highest abilities* through His highest authority.

Chapter Twelve Questions:

1. We don't operate in our own ______________________, but in the ______________________ of Jesus Christ!

2. List 5 attributes of "authority" as it relates to the Lord, in this chapter.

    1.

    2.

    3.

    4.

    5.

3. When can we be used to our highest abilities through His highest authority?

____

____

____

____

____

4. What do I have that I can give back to the Lord?

____

____

____

____

____

____

____

____

____

____

5. Do I want to be loved by the Lord? Am I ready to love His instruction and His correction?

6. As it relates to this chapter, what powerful tool can glorify God tremendously, but can also be used to gratify selfish motives?

7. What passage of scripture shows us the story of Lucifer's pride and fall so that we may keep our feet out of the same snare?

8. What tools must I use to keep my heart and mind cleansed as I repent?

Chapter Thirteen
Being Worship

Worship is never about how to "do." For far too long we have had many people in church week after week, service after service, *doing* worship. *God is requiring us to stop doing worship, and start being worship.* Worship has been, is, and always will be about who to be, not what to do! Worship is not a job. Worship is a persona, a being.

Worship is not about the most talented, or gifted. Worship is not even about music, even though in our society we "show" worship most of the time, at least in our mental images, with the use of music.

Worship is a lifestyle, a way of living, a way of being. Worship is not for a moment, or a season, or a service… not for a performance, or a job. Worship is truly about the soul, mind, spirit, and mostly, the will of the person in which worship is housed. Worship is about dying, dying to self, dying to self-will, dying to wants, desires, anything and everything apart from the very essence of His presence.

There is no such thing, no such position as a worship leader. No one can lead me to worship. If this was true then worship would be a destination, which it is not. Worship is about the heart…the heart in which man cannot see, or feel, or even know. Worship is intimacy, between humankind, and our Creator. Worship is not set aside for a "time frame." Worship is an existence, pure and simple, apart from ourselves, and only for One, our Orchestrator, our Conductor, our Master.

So then, how can we even try to "teach" worship? We can't teach a way of being. So, if worship in itself can't be taught, then how can we have a school of worship? Ah, very good question! It will take me at least a week to tell you, or rather, show you. Hmm... maybe more than a week, maybe a lifetime. A school of worship can no more teach you to be a worshiper than a school of fish can teach someone to be a fish. It is in our desire to gather together, to hear from heaven, to be used by His glory that we can even begin to understand. This so-called school of worship is not a destination. No, rather it is the beginning of a journey, a lifetime journey. Better still, it is an eternal journey. One which we can begin here on earth, right now, but with an arrow on the end of the journey line... a never ending, a never completing, a never completely fulfilling or arriving journey. Why? Because our worship is of an eternal, everlasting God, who is infinite in existence, infinite in performance, infinite in *being,* infinite in understanding, infinite in wisdom... and the list goes on and on... infinitely and into infinity.

Worship in its truest form can be a single note, even a single vocal sound, or a choir of thousands. Worship can be the vibration of one finger on one single key or one plucked string or a symphony of 300 orchestrated musicians. It is not about the masses but about the heart. It is the untrained voice of one crying in the wilderness, or the most gifted and talented of all musicians combined. We have allocated worship in our society to be those who have the "gifts." But that is not our eternal Creator's definition. He looks for the heart of the true worshiper, whose heart is in his giving. He searches the entire earth for the one who worships not out of his head, or his ability, but in spirit and in truth.

Worship is about giving of one's self completely to the Creator. Worship is a way of being, a way of living, and a way of movement. Ah, something new! Movement! Now there is a "doing" word, movement and motion. But when humility, purity, integrity, and accountability are included, when all performance has been removed, all ideas, thoughts, perceptions of my "doing" the motion is completely removed, then what is left for me to do? Nothing, nothing at all. Just be… be still… just be… submitted, used, an instrument of His presence, in total and complete surrender.

Surrender with me, now.

"Let the words of my mouth and the meditation of my heart be acceptable in Your sight, my strength and my redeemer! What can the instrument do apart from the One who is doing the playing? The instrument can do nothing apart from the One. So, here I am Lord, play me. Make me be Your melody, Your lyric, Your sound! Let me be the sound the world hears and recognizes the very existence of an all-powerful God! Let the world hear through me the sound waves of Your love, Your overpowering strength, Your pure and cleansing streams. Lord, use me, play me as Your instrument of pleasure. Let the sound waves of Your presence come forth beckoning, crying out, singing, renewing, reviving, quickening, all who long for You! Let them hear You through me. I have come before You, and I lay myself, this instrument at Your feet. Lord, come down from Your holy habitation, reaching down, and picking me up, into Your hands, Your mighty anointed hands; play the sounds of healing, and restoration. Play the sounds of Your glory, rising, cleansing all who will listen!

I am a woodwind instrument set before You to be played. Without the breath of Your divine presence, no sound of any value or worth can come forth. I am a stringed instrument laid at Your feet. Without Your divine fingers strumming, plucking, running over the reverberations of these yielded strings, no sound can come forth. I am any and all instruments awaiting the glorious and divine touch of Your presence. Without Your touch, I am a clanging cymbal and a sounding brass, a broken and unproductive sound wave that moves no one and goes no where.

Lord, I am Yours. I trust You. I will no longer belong to You part of the time, and myself part of the time. I belong to You. If there is no sound coming from me, then it is the divine Musician who wishes for this silence, not the instrument. This instrument no longer has a will, for I freely give my self, my will, my mind, my body, my instrument to my divine Creator.

May the light of Your glory be seen in me. May the sound of Your presence be heard through me. I am Yours and You are mine. This is My Beloved's song, an eternal love song, but only those who are washed clean by the blood of the Lamb can hear it. Can you hear it? It is the sound of the redeemed crying loudly… even so, "Come, Lord Jesus!"
And the Bridegroom says, "I am coming quickly."
And the Bride says, "Come, Lord, Jesus.
And the Bridegroom says, "I am coming soon."
And the Bride says, "Come, Lord, Jesus."
And the Bridegroom says, "Behold! It is finished; I am coming."
And the Bride says, "Even so, come! Lord, Jesus."

Chapter Thirteen Questions:

1. What is God requiring of us, in regards to worship?

____

____

____

____

____

2. Write in journal form (freely), what you know about worship at this point and reflect on what you thought worship was, before now.

____

____

____

____

____

____

____

____

____

____

____

____

____

____

____

____

____

____

____

____

____

____

____

3. Realize that you are not being "taught worship," you are *becoming worship.* What does this mean to you and how does this deepen your relationship with God?

____

____

____

____

____

4. Pray this prayer of submission often. Your own voice, music, and/or motion of submission and worship will take over as you love your Creator without reservation!

"Let the words of my mouth and the meditation of my heart be acceptable in Your sight, my strength and my redeemer! What can the instrument do apart from the One who is doing the playing? The instrument can do nothing, apart from the One. So, here I am Lord, play me. Make me be Your melody, Your lyric, Your sound! Let me be the sound the world hears and recognizes the very existence of an all-powerful God! Let the world hear through me the sound waves of Your love, Your overpowering strength, Your pure and cleansing streams. Lord, use me, play me as Your instrument of pleasure. Let the sound waves of Your presence come forth beckoning, crying out, singing, renewing, reviving, quickening, all who long for You! Let them hear You through me. I have come before You, and I lay myself, this instrument at Your feet. Lord, come down from Your holy habitation, reach down, and pick me up, into Your hands. May Your mighty anointed hands play the sounds of healing and restoration. Play the sounds of Your glory rising and cleansing all who will listen!

Chapter Fourteen
Restoration of Worship

II Kings 23:1-8

Now the king sent them to gather all the elders of Judah and Jerusalem to him.

The king went up to the house of the Lord with all the men of Judah, and with him all the habitants of Jerusalem - the priests and the prophets and all the people, both small and great. And he read in their hearing all the words of the Book of the Covenant which had been found in the house of the Lord.

Then the king stood by a pillar and made a covenant before the Lord, to follow the Lord and to keep His commandments and His testimonies and His statutes, with all his heart and all his soul, to perform the words of this covenant that were written in this book. And all the people took a stand for the covenant.

And the king commanded Hilkiah the high priest, the priest of the second order, and the doorkeepers, to bring out of the temple of the Lord all the articles that were made for Baal, for Asherah, and for all the host of heaven; and he burned them outside Jerusalem in the field of Kidron, and carried their ashes to Bethel.

Then he removed the idolatrous priests whom the kings of Judah had ordained to burn incense on the high places in the cities of Judah and in the place all around Jerusalem, and those who burned incense to Baal, to the sun, to the moon, to the constellations, and to all the host of heaven.

And he brought out the wooden image from the house of the

Lord, to the Brook Kidron outside Jerusalem, burned it at the Brook Kidron and ground it to ashes, and threw its ashes on the graves of the common people.

Then he tore down the ritual booths of the perverted persons that were in the house of the Lord, where the women wove hangings for the wooden image.

And he brought all the priests from the cities of Judah, and defiled the high places where the priests had burned incense, from Geba to Beersheba; also he broke down the high places at the gates which were at the entrance of the Gate of Joshua the governor of the city, which were to the left of the city gate.

Then in verses 20-25, *He executed all the priests of the high places who were there, on the altars, and burned men's bones on them; and he returned to Jerusalem.*

Then the king commanded all the people, saying, "Keep the Passover to the Lord your God, as it is written in this Book of the Covenant."

Such a Passover surely had never been held since the days of the judges who judged Israel, nor in all the days of the kings of Israel and the kings of Judah.

But in the eighteenth year of King Josiah this Passover was held before the Lord in Jerusalem.

Moreover Josiah put away those who consulted mediums and spiritists, the household gods and idols, all the abominations that were seen in the land of Judah and in Jerusalem, that he might perform the words of the law which were written in the book that Hilkiah the priest found in the house of the Lord.

Now before him there was no king like him, who turned to the Lord with all his heart, with all his soul, and with all his might, according to all the Law of Moses; nor after him did any arise like him.

In this entire chapter, we find a king whose sole purpose was to restore worship, cleanse the altars of God, and bring down those who have opposed God's purified worship. He had a huge job and he went after it with gusto. But if you continue to read, you will find that no matter what he did it was not enough. He could clean up the physical parts of worship but he could not cleanse the heart of the worshipers. Each person in his kingdom had to find his own way to the Lord and to purification. The people were accustomed to doing whatever they felt like in God's house, and the physical actions of destroying the idols, and cleaning house, so to speak, of the unrighteous people in leadership was not enough to change the hearts of the people.

They had been corrupt for generations, and the sins of the forefathers had taken root in the hearts of the present generation and since the Lord is in our future long before we are, God knew that this one king's heart to cleanse the people was not going to be enough. Even though God saw all his efforts the people went virtually unchanged. King Josiah was killed not long after he began the restoration of the house of the Lord. The next king did evil in the sight of the Lord, and so did the next king. The people's lack of repentance and change brought about a very hard time for them. They were heavily taxed by the Pharaoh Necho of Egypt, who had killed the righteous King Josiah.

Restoring worship was not about music, or singers, or dancers, or people. Restoring worship was about restoring God's altars and God's people in purification. Without God's altars being purified and made ready once again, how can those who have purified their hearts come before Him corporately? We start our purification and restoration personally with our hearts toward God's heart. But once that position has been restored and our hearts are made ready before Him, then God's altars, literally, the altars in His places of collective worship must be reopened, purified, and made ready for His people to be able to bring our worship to Him!

We see in this time of King Josiah, that the physical house of the Lord and His altars were made ready but the people did not change. Even when King Josiah made the command for the people to gather and perform the worship of Passover, the people were not changed.

I will keep the altar of my heart purified.

Why am I bringing this to your attention? You are a called and anointed worshiper of the Lord. You are responsible for your own actions and your own heart and mind. You are held accountable to the Lord for what you do, and who you are. If the people follow you, then rejoice. If they do not follow, as in the case with King Josiah, know that you are doing what you are led to do and be. You are to keep your heart right. You are to keep yourself clean and purified by the Lord. You are to stay in His face, and in His fire. What others do is up to them. You can tell them, make it easier for them, but ultimately their own hearts, minds, and lives are set in motion by their own choices.

Can this be discouraging? Absolutely! But you cannot allow this discouragement to stop you from doing what is right. We studied this already in the life of Elijah and his desire for Jezebel to recognize who God is. No matter what happens around us, or even to us, we must stay focused on keeping our own lives in a purified and holy position before the

Lord. This is not a request but a command from the throne of God.

Restoration in worship is essential if we are to move into the higher place of His presence. We long for it. We long for His power and presence made manifest in our gatherings and even in our daily lives. But we will not be able to tap into His greatness without giving Him access to us. He cannot have access to us until we do what is necessary to clean up our altars, our lives. We are His worship; we are His altar.

We must learn to focus on Him, desire Him, long for Him. We must understand the amazing, creative force of the universe who created us is calling for us to come to Him! If we do not come, He will call someone else! That is not acceptable to me! I don't believe it is acceptable to you, either. God is calling us to come to Him, to worship Him in spirit and in truth. His arms are wide open asking us to run to Him, purified by His own gift of His Son's shed blood.

There is no longer any time left to ignore His calling, or to expect someone else to do it. He is calling you! Will you come before Him and be made ready to worship Him? Once Lucifer fell from the presence of God, and forever lost his position of lead worshiper, God created His own image to worship Him. That's you and me. Are we being who we were created to be, or have we fallen into the same rut as Lucifer before his fall? Are we more taken with ourselves than we are captivated by His glory? Are we more interested in what others think of us, than we are concerned with God's thoughts toward us? Are we enthralled with our own abilities, completely missing the point that in the light of His glory we are nothing? In spite of our human tendencies to self-worship, God still has entrusted us with the high-ranking position of worshiper in His kingdom. Will we arise to this challenge or sink back into the self-focus of pride and arrogance, only to leave our most high and awesome God without His due worship?

I will worship Him! I will lay down my life before Him! As He is coming into my life I prepare the way for His entrance. I lay myself down as a highway of worship for Him to ride upon. I cast up a highway of worship and praise as an entrance onto the freeway of the Spirit of God.

Just imagine the phrase in Isaiah 40 and then again in the mouth of John the Baptist, *"Prepare the way of the Lord!"* We are to prepare the entrance of the Lord into our lives. We are to make an on-ramp, so to speak, onto the highway we long to ride upon into His presence! The highway is there already but until we build an on-ramp in our lives through praise and worship, we cannot access it.

Will you get yourself ready, purify yourself, and make ready the way of the Lord in your life? This is what He is asking of us, and if we will not do it, I believe with all my heart, that He will simply move on to the one who will. I do not want to be left behind by the Spirit of God as He searches the whole earth over for those who will worship Him in spirit and truth, only to come to me and find me only concerned with myself, my ways, my problems. I want Him to find me all about His business, all about Him. I want Him to find me already worshiping Him through my spirit and in truth. I want Him to find me cleansed by the blood of His Son and my Savior, Jesus Christ. I want Him to find me operating in complete and total truth, denying all flesh existence in my life.

Chapter Fourteen Questions:

1. What was King Josiah's sole purpose?

2. In order for worship to be restored, what must be cleansed and made ready, after our hearts and lives have been cleansed and made ready?

3. Once I am cleansed, purified, sanctified and made ready to become worship to my Lord, who am I responsible for at that point? (Even as an appointed worship leader/team member.)

4. What will God do if I do not come when He calls?

5. Am I more taken with myself than I am captivated by His glory?

6. How do we access the "highway" into His presence?

7. When the Lord searches the whole earth over, looking for those who will worship Him in spirit and truth, what will He find when His eyes rest upon me?

Chapter Fifteen
Heaven and Earth Worship

Revelation 5:9-13

And they sang a new song, saying:

> *"You are worthy to take the scroll, and to open its seals;*
> *For You were slain, and have redeemed us to God by Your blood*
> *Out of every tribe and tongue and people and nation,*
> *And have made us kings and priests to our God;*
> *And we shall reign on the earth."*

Then I looked, and I heard the voice of many angels around the throne, the living creatures, and the elders; and the number of them was ten thousand times ten thousand, and thousands of thousands,

saying with a loud voice:

> *"Worthy is the Lamb who was slain*
> *To receive power and riches and wisdom,*
> *And strength and honor and glory and blessing!"*

And every creature which is in heaven and on the earth and under the earth and such as are in the sea, and all that are in them, I heard saying:

> *"Blessing and honor and glory and power*
> *Be to Him who sits on the throne,*
> *And to the Lamb, forever and ever!"*

We are in training on the earth for who we are now, and for who we will forever be. If we think that this has anything to do with our comfort here then we are grossly mistaken. God is much more interested in our character than our comfort. He is much more interested in our being holy than He is in making us happy. He is not coming back for a bride still in the crib needing constant attention, crying for someone to come and put the pacifier back in the mouth that had just spit it out! He is coming for a mature bride, one who has been made ready for Him, and is mature enough to be His bride.

It is not as if we have not been given enough time! We have been given more than enough time, more than enough warnings, more than enough watchmen on the walls of our lives who have continually been yelling, "Behold, the Bridegroom cometh!" We must be prepared and made ready. There is so little time left for preparation. Have you trimmed the wick of your life and heart? Have you continued to keep your lamp lit? Have you continued to buy enough oil as you wait for His appearing? If not, get busy, and do it quickly! Get on your face and repent, and be made ready! Jesus, our Bridegroom is coming! Heaven's worship is all about Him. Our worship must be all about Him. He is worthy!

Lucifer was made with musical instruments within him. Ezekiel 28:13 states that "tambourines and flutes" were a part of his physical being. But in Isaiah 14:11-15 we read, *Your pomp is brought down to Sheol, and the sound of your stringed instruments; the maggot is spread under you, and worms cover you. How you are fallen from heaven, O Lucifer, son of the morning! How you are cut down to the ground, you who weakened the nations! For you have said in your heart: 'I will ascend into heaven, I will exalt my throne above the stars of God; I will also sit on the mount of the congregation on the farthest sides of the north; I will ascend above the heights of the clouds, I will be like the Most High.' Yet you shall be brought down to Sheol, to the lowest depths of the Pit.*

Being prideful within our own abilities will cause a great fall from positioning within the ranks of God's kingdom. This is not a warning or a threat. This is a fact. The precedent has already been set. Judgment has already been pronounced and sentencing has been carried out for the highest angel in charge of worship. To be so prideful as to think this would never happen to you is being presumptuous and even more prideful! We must guard against such a horrible attack of our minds and hearts. For every called and appointed worshiper, especially those with giftings, and callings and talents, this luciferian spirit is the greatest of all life's temptations.

You know the old saying, "Misery loves company." Well, it certainly applies here. Satan, formerly Lucifer, the son of the morning, has already been cast down. Now his greatest challenge is to have company! His biggest and ever present challenge is to get his "replacements" to make the same mistakes he made and cause them to fall also. This is a constant and ever present temptation and to think that we ever "get over it" is the highest level of stupidity. For to think that this is something that eventually Satan will simply give up on and walk away from you is beyond childish. This kind of thinking is already in a fallen state. The one who thinks, "This could never happen to me," has already fallen prey to the pride and is so deep within it, that the mask of pride they wear is not even visible to their own eyes! We must repent and stay in a repentant mode. We cannot become so taken with even our knowledge of the situation as to think we could not be tempted away. That very thought tells me you have already been tempted away and you have given in to this temptation.

I know this is ever ongoing, an onslaught on the minds and hearts of worshipers over the earth. Satan does not want you to succeed in wearing your garment of praise and your robe of righteousness. He wants you to think that these coverings are not sufficient enough to show His glory, when in actuality, he has already convinced our minds that these coverings are not sufficient enough to show *our glory*. We have been deceived! We must stay low, and get over ourselves. We must come before Him with a broken and humble heart. There is no other way. This is the calling of His worshipers, those for whom His eyes are searching, within the entire earth!

Living the life of a humble worshiper is much like trying to breathe in an all-consuming fire. For generations, firemen have taught us these three steps: 1. Stop! 2. Drop! 3. Roll!

In our lives as worshipers these same three rules apply. We must continually learn to *stop* what we are doing, and begin to understand the purpose of our creation. We must *drop* to our knees to repent, and then to our faces to worship Him in spirit and truth. We must learn to *roll* everything, I mean everything, on Him for He cares for us. We cannot think that we are capable of doing anything worthy enough on our own to stand up in His presence. We must totally rely upon the work of the Spirit of God within us. As we learn to stay low, very low, we learn that in a fire, all the oxygen is in the lower part of the room. The same applies in the realm of the spirit. When we learn to humble ourselves, and get as low as possible, not only is it hard to see us anymore, but there is life down low - there is air to breathe… oxygen of the Spirit of God that can save us!

To be a worshiper who will be found by God, we must learn to practice this method of survival regularly. Stop! Drop! Roll! When you do this, look for me; I will be down there with you at His feet.

Chapter Fifteen Questions:

1. What kind of bride will the Lord be returning to find?

2. What must I do if I am not ready? When?

3. As it relates to this chapter, being prideful can cause what?

4. How can I keep myself from falling prey to pride?

5. If I am thinking, "Pride? No way! Not me!" then what must I do immediately?

6. This earthly life is training me for what?

7. Three keys to living the life of a humble worshiper are what?

1.

2.

3.

Chapter Sixteen
Wordless Worship and Weeping Worship

There is a place for silent worship but this is not what I am referring to here. I am not talking about worship without sounds. I am talking about worship without words! Have you ever been to a place in your life when you were so broken, so hurt, so depressed, so lost in grief that when you approached the throne of God to worship, no words would come forth? We have been there, not once or twice but many times. For different seasons in our lives we find we need different seasons of worship. When we are elated by some victory we can shout and dance and spin and twirl! When we are comfortable and life is going smoothly we can lift our hands and sing sweet, lovely and beautiful songs before the Lord. But when all hell has broken lose in our lives and we have lost all ability within ourselves to verbalize the condition of our hearts we need to learn that God accepts our worship even without human words of understanding.

Groaning and Sighing.

II Corinthians 5:4
For while we are still in this tent, we groan under the burden and sigh deeply (weighed down, depressed, oppressed) - not that we want to put off the body (the clothing of the spirit), but rather that we would be further clothed, so that what is mortal (our dying body) may be swallowed up by life [after the resurrection]. (Amplified Bible)

What an amazing scripture in description of who we really are. We are a spirit and we are clothed in this flesh body. Our flesh body is called the "tent" or "house" of who we really are; we are a spirit. Our spirit groans under the weight of these flesh bodies. Our spirits long to worship the Lord of lords. Our spirit is strong; our flesh is weak! So then how do we become the worship He deserves? We overcome our flesh by building up our spirit beings.

II Timothy 1:6 tells us, "to stir up the gift of God within us." The gift of God within us is the gift of the Holy Spirit. We don't need to stir up the Holy Spirit! He does not need to be stirred up, but the giftings within us need to be stirred up. Why? Because they become dormant, or settle down. When Paul wrote Timothy this letter it was because Timothy was becoming discouraged over what some were saying about him. He was young for the position he had been given by the Spirit of God. Paul had gotten wind of these discouraging statements that had been made so he wrote Timothy a letter telling him to get over what people were saying about him. He needed to stir up the gifts of God within him. "Gifts" in this particular passage of scripture is the Greek word "charisma." It is not the same Greek word for "gift" used in I Corinthians 12, which is "dorea." Dorea is the Greek word for gift that means "the gift that gives." That is the gift of the Holy Spirit. The Holy Spirit is the gift that gives gifts to us! The gifts that the Holy Spirit gives to us is the Greek word "charisma." This is what Paul was telling Timothy to stir up - these gifts of the Spirit of God within him. Then Paul followed that statement with the all-famous words, *For God has not given us a spirit of fear, but of power and of love and of a sound mind.* (II Timothy 1:7)

Weeping.

Psalm 6:6-10
I am weary with my groaning; all night I soak my pillow with tears. I drench my couch with my weeping. My eye grows dim because of grief; it grows old because of all my enemies. Depart from me, all you workers of iniquity, for the Lord has heard the voice of my weeping. The Lord has

heard my supplication; the Lord receives my prayer. Let all my enemies be ashamed and sorely troubled; let them turn back and be put to shame suddenly. (Amplified Bible)

There are times in our worship that it turns from worship to prayer. Sometimes when we start praying we wind up worshiping. Prayer and worship many times go hand in hand and can intertwine back and forth like the interweaving of a blanket. It can be comforting and encouraging to us; then at other times, we can be so brokenhearted as we worship and pray that we simply run out of understandable words to pray or sing, and we find ourselves bent down, holding our mid-section groaning with an exhausting overwhelming sense of His presence. It can leave our flesh spent, or as Isaiah said in chapter six, *"I am undone."*

John 11:38
Then Jesus, again groaning in Himself, came to the tomb. It was a cave, and a stone lay against it.

When Jesus was at Lazarus' tomb He sighed and groaned not because of the grief of Lazarus being dead, or from the weight of His work to believe for His resurrection. He was groaning because the lack of faith of the people who were supposed to know Him so well by that point. I believe He sighed like many of us sigh when we thought we were at a certain point in our lives of faith only to fall once again at the same place fighting with our flesh!

Romans 8:23
And not only the creation, but we ourselves too, who have and enjoy the first fruits of the [Holy] Spirit [a foretaste of the blissful things to come] groan inwardly as we wait for the redemption of our bodies [from sensuality and the grave, which will reveal] our adoption (our manifestation as God's sons.) (Amplified Bible)

> *Whether in laughter or tears ... I will worship You.*

Sometimes in our pursuit of His presence we get to the point where we cannot continue on without a new touch from the Lord, a new revelation, a new anointing of His presence. There are things that happen in our lives that can cause us to want to give up and stop living. But we cannot give up, for if we give up on Tuesday, then there is no Wednesday. It is not about always understanding the journey or even the destination, but about the pursuit that is a lifestyle of living. Worship is not meant to be a time within a service. Worship is not meant to be contained within the music portion of any given service. Worship is about a lifestyle of pursuing Him. Worship is about Him, His presence and the choices we make to continue on in this wonderful pursuit.

We have become so good at worshiping for the audience, but we have not spent enough time in preparation worshiping for the only One who should be listening. Everyone who is in a worship service should come to worship, to participate in the worship, not to be entertained by those on the platform.

When all else cannot seem to reach the place within Him that we long for, many times the only way to worship Him in spirit and truth is in silence. *Be still and know that He is God.* (Psalm 46:10). Sometimes being silent before Him is the ultimate of comfort in His presence. Harry and I have been married for 24 years and it did not happen right away. In fact, I am not certain when it happened but years into our relationship, I realized one day while riding in the car for hours that we had ridden for hundreds of miles and had not said one word. The realization was not of the silence but of the comfortableness of this silence. The truth of this level of intimacy was that we were so comfortable being together that we did not have to fill up the space around us with words; in fact, no words were necessary at all. We knew how we felt about each other; we did not have to say anything at all. There was nothing more precious than the comfort of silence between us. It was beautiful.

When we get to the point in our worship when we are as comfortable in total silence or weeping tears of worship, as we are when we are shouting, dancing, and singing, then we can be assured we have reached a beautiful level of intimacy in our worship. Whether the Spirit says anything or not, is not important. We are together, we who worship, and the One and only true God, who is being worshiped.

I have had times in my life when silence and tears have been the consistent components in my worship.

Psalm 126:5-6
Those who sow in tears shall reap in joy. He who continually goes forth weeping, bearing seed for sowing, shall doubtless come again with rejoicing, bringing his sheaves with him.

Psalm 56:8-9
You number my wanderings; Put my tears into Your bottle; Are they not in Your book? When I cry out to You, then my enemies will turn back; This I know, because God is for me.

Psalm 34:17-18
The righteous cry out, and the Lord hears, and delivers them out of all of their troubles. The Lord is near to those who have a broken heart, and saves such as have a contrite spirit.

The *Message Bible* reads, in Psalm 34:9-11, *Worship God if you want the best; worship opens doors to all his goodness. Young lions on the prowl get hungry, but God-seekers are full of God. Come, children, listen closely; I'll give you a lesson in God worship.*

I am always looking for lessons in God worship. Here is one spelled out in God's Word. I think it is an easy thing to answer that all humans want the best for their lives. The above verse states that if we want the best we are to worship God. Worshiping God opens the doors to all His goodness. People who seek God are full of God! What a statement that is! When we choose to worship God, and we come to Him and listen closely, we receive instruction from the throne of God.

There have been times in my life when all I could do was cry at His feet. There were even those moments of crisis when my tears were so heavy that they literally choked the words right out of me! No more words that could be understood by human ears would proceed from my mouth. Only cries and groans and moans of my spirit to the Spirit could be identified from my being. Was God offended by my lowly state of worship? Not at all!

In the *Message Bible,* I love the way Psalm 34:15 reads, *God keeps an eye on his friends, his ears pick up every moan and groan.*

God is not insulted or offended when our worship goes beyond our humanness. In fact, I see in His Word that when we get to this point of unexplainable worship, no more words in intellect, He promises to be listening. He hears what we cannot say. He hears what we cannot think or even imagine. He hears the very cries of our hearts!

In Malachi 3:16-18, *Then those who feared the Lord spoke to one another, and the Lord listened and heard them; so a book of remembrance was written before Him for those who fear the Lord and who meditate on His name. "They shall be Mine," says the Lord of hosts, "On the day that I make them My jewels. And I will spare them as a man spares his own son who serves him." Then you shall again discern between the righteous and the wicked, between the one who serves God and one who does not serve Him.*

The Lord is listening to those who fear the Lord. He listens even when we speak to one another! If we fear Him, He is listening to us, and He is writing down our words in a book of remembrance! That could only mean that He does not miss a thing and our words are important enough for Him to log in a book to remember them, act upon them, and utilize them in the form of prayers. Just to know that the Lord God Almighty is listening is powerful enough, but to realize that He is recording our words in a book to remember! This is powerful. We need to be careful what we say, because it is logged for eternity in a book!

There are times when our worship is filled with joy. Then there are other times when it is filled with sorrow. There are times when we want to dance, and then there are other times when we lay in a heap at His feet, exhausted and spent. The point is that no matter what our condition we bring it to Him! We must never turn away from Him but we must always run to Him!

After our daughter died in 1999, I didn't run from the Lord or from worship but my worship changed. It became about what I could not say. It became about much moaning and groaning and a lot of tears. I never felt the Lord reject my worship no matter what form it was presented in because He knows my heart. My heart was to never stop worshiping

Him! I said my worship changed, but it did not stop. I need you to hear that statement. For some of you, when you got to the point in your situations and circumstances that you felt completely out of control and had no idea the outcome, many times you have pulled back away from the Father God. This is the time when you must press into the Father God for He knows you far better than you know yourself. Don't be afraid to be real with the Lord! Charles Spurgeon once said, "Tears are like liquid prayers that carry a lot of weight at the throne of grace." Never could there be a more true statement than this. Prayers that are said through the choking sounds of tears are the most powerful of prayers at His feet.

Remember in Psalm 56 how God catches our tears in a bottle! Our tears are so important that not one falls without notice from the throne of grace. Tears that fall from a humble and broken heart are a myriad of prayers to the throne of God. In Exodus 3:7, *And the Lord said; "I have surely seen the oppression of My people who are in Egypt, and have heard their cry because of their taskmasters, for I know their sorrows."* The Lord is always listening and He hears, and He knows. The scripture here says plainly that the Lord knows our sorrows.

The word "know" in Hebrew is the word, "yada" and is pronounced (yah-dah). It is in the *Strong's Concordance* as #3045 and means "to know, to perceive, to distinguish, to recognize, to acknowledge, to be acquainted with;" in a few instances to "know intimately, that is, sexually, also to acknowledge, recognize, esteem, and endorse." When the scripture speaks of God's making known His name, it refers to His revealing (through deeds or events) what His name *truly means.* Thus, in Exodus 6:3, *I appeared to Abraham, to Isaac, and to Jacob as El Shaddai (God Almighty), but by My name Yahweh (LORD) I was not known to them.* God did not mean that the Patriarchs had never heard the name

Yahweh, but rather that He did not reveal the full meaning of His name, Yahweh, until the time of Moses and the Exodus. (Word Wealth, *Spirit-Filled Life Bible*).

II Kings 20:5-6
...Thus says the Lord, the God of David your father, "I have heard your prayer, I have seen your tears; surely I will heal you. On the third day you shall go up to the house of the Lord. And I will add to your days fifteen years. I will deliver you and this city from the hand of the king of Assyria; and I will defend this city for My own sake, and for the sake of My servant David."

King Hezekiah had been given a death sentence by the prophet Isaiah that he was about to die. The king cried out to God in prayer and he wept bitterly before the Lord, the Bible says in verse three. So the Lord spoke again through the prophet Isaiah and gave the king another chance with a promise of 15 more years to his life. What I want you to notice is when the Lord spoke to the king, He told him that He had heard his prayers and had seen his tears. God does not miss anything! He hears us because He listens, and He also sees us! He knows when we are truly broken before Him. He knows when we are cloaked in humility or just pretending to be humble. He knows us! Intimately! We cannot fool God!

So in conclusion, what can I say? There is no end to worship, for how can there be? There is no end to our God, so there can never be an end to His worship. We must be ever learning, growing, and transforming in His presence. We must be ever becoming more like Him and less like us! We must ever be worshiping Him. We must ever *be worship* for Him! So there is no end, only pursuit; pursuit of His presence, pursuit of who He is. We run after Him and He delights in us! He laughs and sighs and holds us. He longs for us, and aches for us to simply come before His presence with singing, entering His gates with praise! Will you join me in this lifelong pursuit of His glory? If so, I will meet you once again at His feet. This is where we belong, where we fit, and where we truly can be His worship!

I worship You, Lord,
from the depths of my spirit –
– even when words
cannot be found.

Chapter Sixteen Questions:

1. What am I being told to stir up, in II Timothy 1:6?

2. When my audible, intelligible worship turns to unintelligible groans, am I still worshiping?

3. Is it possible to worship God in complete silence?

4. Is the Lord listening, even when all I can do is weep before Him? Is He insulted by this "lowly worship?"

5. What must I always do, even when I am sorrowful, angry or exhausted?

____
____
____
____
____
____

6. Where do we who worship, truly belong?

____
____
____
____
____
____

7. The Lord God Almighty, Yahweh, hears my cries, sees my tears, and even keeps them for me. Never have I known such love in the natural. I will journal the intimacies inside my heart, of my love for Him. *I desire to be Your worship…*

____
____
____
____
____
____
____
____
____
____
____
____
____
____
____

Chapter Seventeen
Prophetic Vision of Worship

In the many decades that I have been at His feet in worship, there have been times when I have felt like John the Revelator, or Daniel, or Ezekiel. I have seen visions as clearly and as memorable as an earthly event witnessed with my natural eyes and mind. As this school of worship has been developing in the womb of my spirit, and as this *We Who Worship* book has been birthed in my being, through deep prayer and intercession, there have been supernatural manifestations of time, space, events, if you will, that have unfolded before my spirit's eyes.

As I was in prayer before the Lord over these pages being written, I saw something. Things of the spirit are many times hard to describe in our lower, slower language. I will do my very best with my limited verbal skills to describe the events and details of what I have seen. If only we could write in the heavenly language of tongues and the reader could pray and receive the interpretation through the Spirit of God! Maybe for a time in the future but for now I will make an attempt at this lower level of sound, time, and space.

I was hovering over the curve of the earth in a desert place. There was a dead sea of sorts, mountains, hills, flat in between, dry, very dry. There was death everywhere but it was so intermingled amongst the people that they did not seem to notice the stench of death all over them. They were moving around, going about their daily routines, some were laughing at nothing, nonsense in the presence and purpose of Almighty God. Others were non-feeling, almost zombie-like in their motions, like the walking dead. Others were broken and crying, too weak to continue trying to make

any sounds. I was being taken up higher so I could see from the beginning to the end. As I continued to pray by the Spirit of God, my eyes began to adjust to all I was seeing at once and I noticed something lying across the entire valley, across the desert floor. It was lying like a winding rope, snaking its way across the entire valley. Neither end of this "thing" could be seen. It was as if it had neither a beginning nor an end. It was huge, beyond description in size. It lay like a Great Wall of China, miles and miles in the distance in both directions, lying as if dead, but not dead… only dormant. It was wide enough to walk upon, to ride upon in several vehicles at once. It was impenetrable, strong, and secure. It was immoveable, set in place as if it had taken possession of the land on which it lay.

My eyes adjusted even more and I noticed it had scales, like some sort of reptilian creature, but it looked petrified. No fluid, no water seemed present in its existence. It indeed looked completely dead, void of all life, huge but harmless just lying across the many miles of desert sand. People were all over it, climbing, driving, etc. with no fear or notice of it at all. It had been there so long, that humans had become accustomed to it being a part of their everyday lives.

As I looked closer, fear began to grip my being and I began to whisper as I prayed to the Lord to show me what this was, lying so seemingly innocent across this dry, desert place. I whispered in prayer, "Lord, what is this? What am I seeing? What are You showing me?" The Lord quieted my spirit and told me, "Do not be afraid. Look closely."

As I peered at this thing I saw a slight shimmer, a movement beneath the moving feet of the unsuspecting

and unprepared people. It only appeared to be lifeless. It was as if it slightly shook, almost like the big ol' ugly thing shivered. As I stared at this huge and still growing, horrible thing, I saw its scales just slightly opening up, and without even one person closest to it noticing, I saw eyes! It had eyes all over it, lots of ugly, yellow, devilish eyes showing itself as the predator it was, lying in wait for the unsuspecting to come even closer to it.

I wanted to scream to the people to get away from this hideous and insidious creature! I felt myself yelling to the people to wake up and look up! Notice what is right there beside you!!!! Yet, no matter how much I screamed and yelled, all the sounds coming forth from my being seemed to fall on deaf ears.

I frantically turned to the Lord who was looking on this scene unfolding before my eyes. I cried out to the Lord to help me sound the alarm! "Help me, Lord, to reach the people in time. Help me to help them!" He quickly and quietly touched me and said, "You obey Me. It will be what it will be."

With those words, I was once again sitting in my morning prayer chair. It has taken me months to get to the point of trying to write this in our language of earthly words. I cannot even try and interpret what this is. I do not feel the Lord telling me to try and explain it. After months of praying in the spirit, I am only certain of one thing. Worship can break the power of this thing. I don't know how, or when, but I know worship can bring it to a halt in the spirit. That's all I know for sure. I hear the Spirit of the Lord saying over and over, "It will be what it will be." I guess the rest is up to you to pray and hear from heaven. I believe this will be what it will be for each one who reads this. I believe the Spirit of God will speak directly to the heart of each individual and line upon line, precept upon precept, thought upon thought, prayer upon prayer, He will reveal by His Spirit what we are to know, when we are to know it.

It will be what it will be!

Overview Questions:

1. After reading this book how do I feel about worship?

2. How will I approach the throne of God, in my private prayer time, differently than I have before?

3. When I gather with other believers to worship God, what can I give to Him that no one else can?

4. When I enter into corporate worship, will I need anyone to lead me?

____
____
____
____
____
____

5. I understand that my gift is never to be compared to someone else's gift, for my worship is not about my gift, but about my ____________________.

6. The Lord showed Cheryl a vision. He allowed her to write it in this book and I have read it. What does this vision mean to me?

____
____
____
____
____
____

7. The Lord wants to show visions to His people. Lord, speak to me. I am listening.

____
____
____
____
____
____
____
____

"It will be what it will be."

I am watching and listening, Lord.

Use me.

I am Your worship.

Prayer of Salvation

If you have never made Jesus the Lord of your life, or if you would like to re-dedicate your life to Him, please pray this prayer of salvation.

Heavenly Father, I come to You admitting that I am a sinner. Right now, I choose to turn away from sin and I ask You to cleanse me of all unrighteousness. I believe that Your Son, Jesus, died on the cross to take away my sins. I also believe that He rose again from the dead so that I might be forgiven of my sins and be made righteous through faith in Him. I call upon the name of Jesus Christ to be the Lord and Savior of my life. Jesus, I choose to follow You and I ask that You fill me with the power of the Holy Spirit. I declare right now that I am a child of God! I am free from sin and full of the righteousness of God. I am saved, in Jesus' name. Amen.

Please contact us to let us know you prayed this prayer!

Salem Family Ministries
PO Box 701287
Tulsa, Oklahoma 74170
salemfamilyministries.org

Please include your prayer requests
and comments when you write.

About the Author

Cheryl Salem walked the runway to become Miss America 1980, despite what appeared to be all odds stacked against her. A horrific car crash resulting in a physical handicap and over 100 stitches in her face were no match for what God had planned for her life. Through simple, childlike faith in Him, she overcame the obstacles and eventually took the crown in Atlantic City! She has used this distinction as a springboard to launch the Gospel of Jesus Christ into churches, schools, women's retreats, television appearances, etc. Numerous ministries, women's shelters, inner-city outreaches and disaster relief programs have made use of Cheryl's books and CD's to offer hope and help to those in need. According to Cheryl, *"None of these things would be possible, if not for my Jesus."*

The Spirit of God is flowing through Cheryl in an amazing way as He leads her to minister in a fascinating, prophetic way that involves a flow of music and teaching that is sung, instead of spoken. This move of the Holy Spirit is touching people at the very core of their being as He gently ministers to them, as deep calls out to deep (Psalm 42:7).

Both Harry and Cheryl Salem are sought-after speakers, who minister at churches and events across the nation. Harry has a heart for men, preaching and teaching on overcoming issues in life. Cheryl is a popular speaker at ladies events, encouraging women to reach their godly potential, but the central focus of Salem Family Ministries is to take this unique, tag-team style of ministry into churches, two by two, to reach families for God, one by one (Luke 10:1-2).

Salem Family Ministries, PO Box 701287, Tulsa, OK 74170

salemfamilyministries.org

References

Joyner, Rick. *The Final Quest* (MorningStar Publications, 1996) *www.MorningStarMinistries.org.* pp 53-55.

Seekins, Frank. *Hebrew Word Pictures* (Living Word Pictures, Inc., 1994).

Strong, James. *Abingdon's Strong's Exhaustive Concordance of the Bibl*e (Nashville: Abingdon, 1980).

Please note: To those of you who read this book or any of our books, the views and opinions expressed are based upon our personal lives and on our own interpretation of the Bible.

Other Available Books

Entering Rest – Be Still... A 40-Day Journey into the Presence of God
Obtaining Peace – A 40-Day Prayer Journal
2 Becoming 1
The Choice is Yours
Overcoming Fear – A 40-Day Prayer Journal
Every Body Needs Balance
From Grief to Glory
From Mourning to Morning
Distractions from Destiny
Speak the Word Over Your Family for Finances
Speak the Word Over Your Family for Healing
Speak the Word Over Your Family for Salvation
Covenant Conquerors
Warriors of the Word
*Fight in the Heavenlies**
*It's Too Soon to Give Up**
Being #1 at Being #2
For Men Only
An Angel's Touch
A Royal Child
The Mommy Book
*How to Get a Balanced Body**
*Simple Facts; Salvation, Healing & the Holy Ghost**
*Health & Beauty Secrets**
*Choose to be Happy**
Abuse... Bruised but not Broken
You Are Somebody
A Bright Shining Place – The Story of a Miracle
*Currently out of print.

To order any of these titles or to submit a prayer request or a praise report, please contact us:

salemfamilyministries.org